C000301677

Flying from Derry

Eglinton & Naval Aviation in Northern Ireland

THE ULSTER AVIATION SOCIETY

© Guy Warner 2007

5 4 3 2 1

All rights reserved. No part of this publication may be reproduced, stored in a retrieval system or transmitted in any form or by any means, electronic, mechanical, photocopying, scanning, recording or otherwise, without the prior written permission of the copyright owners and publisher of this book.

Guy Warner has been a regular contributor to Ulster Airmail, the journal of the Ulster Aviation Society for whom he is also a committe member.

As well as writing for *Aeroplane, Aircraft Illustrated, Air Enthusiast, Airliner World, Air Pictorial, Airways, Aviation Ireland, Air International, Army Air Corps Journal, Aviation News, Flying in Ireland, Flypast, History Ireland, Northern Ireland Travel News, Spirit of the Air* and *230 Squadron Association Newsletter*, he has also had several books published.

He is co-author of *In the Heart of the City: The History of Belfast's City Airport, 1938–1998, Flying from Malone: Belfast's First Civil Aerodrome, Belfast International Airport: Aviation at Aldergrove since 1938, Army Aviation in Ulster, The History of No 72 Squadron RAF* and author of *Blandford to Baghdad: The Story of No 72 Squadron's First CO, The Westland Wessex 1963-2003: 40 Years of RAF Service, Orkney By Air: A Photograpic Journey Through Time, No. 230 Squadron Royal Air Force: Kita Chari Jauh – We Search Far* and *Airships Over the North Channel*.

Guy is married with two daughters and lives in Co Antrim.

Designed by April Sky Design, Newtownards

www.aprilsky.co.uk

CONTENTS

— ∘O∘ —

Guard duty at RNAS Eglinton in the 1950s.
(Author's Collection)

LOCATION MAP

— ∘O∘ —

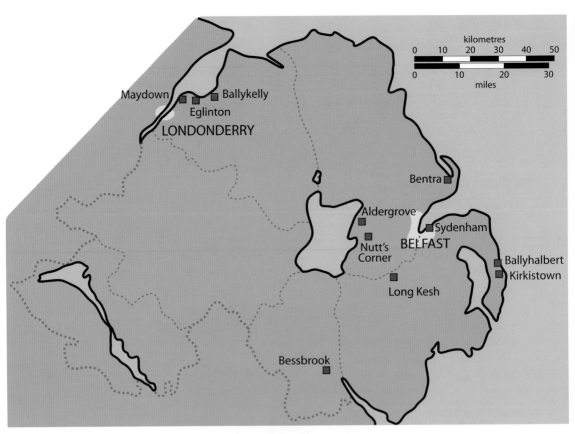

Map of Northern Ireland showing the main locations mentioned in the text.

FOREWORD

— ∘O∘ —

I was delighted to be asked to contribute the foreword to this book, which is much more than just the story of an airfield. For many people throughout the Northwest, the Royal Navy and Fleet Air Arm were welcome guests for many years in times of peace and war. That warm welcome was reciprocated by the men and women of the RN and WRNS who served in Northern Ireland, many of whom came to love its scenic beauty, enjoy its social life and appreciate the friendliness of the local people.

One of the most enjoyable aspects of the book is contained in the personal accounts which the author has gathered together, all of which speak warmly of Eglinton as having a special atmosphere, which is still remembered very fondly to this day.

The story of naval aviation in Northern Ireland was not, of course, just confined to Eglinton and the book covers the other locations fully, taking the story from the first decades of the 20th century to the present day. I commend this book to the reader not just as a volume of military or aviation history but also as a slice of social history which can also be read with enjoyment by those whose interest is not simply aeroplanes and flying.

Mayor, Councillor Helen Quigley

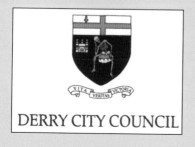

DERRY CITY COUNCIL

APPRECIATION

— ∞o —

Grateful thanks are due to the following for their support:

BAE Systems, Belfast Harbour Commissioners, Belfast International Airport, Belfast Telegraph, Bombardier Aerospace Belfast, Derry City Council, Esme Mitchell Trust, Fleet Air Arm Museum, Irish News, Lisburn City Council, Lord O'Neill Charitable Trust, Milibern Trust, Martin-Baker Aircraft Co. Ltd, North Eastern Education & Library Board, The Honourable the Irish Society, Ulster Aviation Society, Ulster Local History Trust. Special thanks are due, as always to my wife, Lynda.

The author and the Ulster Aviation Society would like to express their sincere thanks to Malcolm and Wesley Johnston of April Sky Design for their excellent work and creative input.

Front Cover:
Lt Cdr Eric Meadowcroft flew two rescue missions to the Dutch freighter Saba on 9th December 1957 in the Dragonfly 916 firstly with CPO Ruddock and then with PO Childs (Lt Cdr E Meadowcroft via Raymond Burrows Collection).

Back Cover (top to bottom):
Fairey Swordfish Mk II LS326, L Flight 836 NAS, now with the Royal Navy Historic Flight (RNHF).
Wessex HAS Mk 3 XP118 at Ballykelly in 1969 (Hugh McGrattan).
Painting of a Short Sturgeon flying over Sydenham and Belfast Harbour by Tom Brown (photographed by Eric Gray).

INTRODUCTION

— ∞o —

The central part of this account focuses on the activities at HMS *Gannet*, the Royal Naval Air Station Eglinton in the period between the end of the Second World War in 1945 and its final closure in February 1963. It was undoubtedly the major Naval Air Station in Northern Ireland not just for the personnel who served there or because of the importance of its functions - it was also a vital and living part of the local economy, which made a vibrant contribution to the life of the area. However, all other important aspects of naval aviation in the Province are also covered. The events of the First World War at Bentra are outlined (and are described in detail in a companion book - Airships over the North Channel). World War Two brought a considerable expansion of bases, activities at all of these are outlined – including Maydown, Eglinton, Sydenham, Long Kesh, Ballyhalbert, Kirkiston and Nutts Corner. Post-war events at Sydenham (where many naval aircraft were maintained,

A Sopwith Ship's Camel 2F.1 mounted on the forward 6 inch gun of HMS Caroline. (HMS Caroline)

converted and repaired) and Ballykelly are also recorded. Not forgotten are the naval aircraft constructed at Short Brothers and test flown from Sydenham and the aircraft carriers built by Harland and Wolff. The final section concerns Royal Navy and Royal Marine helicopters in the Province from 1970 to 2002, which flew from Sydenham, Aldergrove, Long Kesh and Ballykelly.

The most significant Royal Naval presence in Northern Ireland nowadays is HMS *Caroline*, the Headquarters of the Ulster Division Royal Naval Reserve, which is moored by the Alexandra Dock in Belfast Harbour and is the RN's second oldest commissioned warship. It is also the only known survivor of the Battle of Jutland. In 1924 it was converted at Harland and Wolff for its present task but before that time it was involved in a series of trials which have their own place in the history of naval aviation. A launching platform was constructed on the fo'c'sle over the six inch gun, from which a Sopwith 2F.1 Ship's Camel could be launched. Between March and October 1918 N6637, N6768, N6831, N7108 and N7121 are known to have been allocated to *Caroline*. In all, 22 light cruisers of the Grand Fleet had been so equipped by the end of the war. This innovation was not popular with the Captain, according to the pilot, Flight Sub-Lieutenant Hugh Petty RNAS, as the Camel's rotary engine, which was lubricated by castor oil, sprayed copious amounts of it over the ship's paintwork while the engine was being run up prior to take-off.

Ship's Camel taking off from HMS Caroline. (HMS Caroline)

CHAPTER 1

—— ∞∞ ——

WORLD WAR ONE

BENTRA - NEAR WHITEHEAD, CO ANTRIM

During the Great War twenty-three airfields and airship bases were established in Ireland for the Royal Flying Corps (RFC), Royal Naval Air Service (RNAS), US Naval Air Service and Royal Air Force (RAF). The first dedicated aviation facility in Ulster belonged to the RNAS, it was the 150 feet long airship shed at Bentra, which was erected in spring 1917. Coastal patrol airships of the SS and SSZ Classes which were based at RNAS Luce Bay near Stranraer used it as a mooring-out station. A regular duty of the airships from August 1915 was to escort the Larne - Stranraer ferry, *Princess Maud*, as well as mounting convoy escort,

The Princess Maud on Lough Ryan with an escorting airship in 1917. (Donnie Nelson Collection)

anti-U-boat and mine-hunting patrols. The area covered by this aerial surveillance ranged from Carlingford Lough to Ballykelly. It is possible that RNAS fixed-wing aircraft visited Bentra too, the site was known locally during the war years as the Aerodrome and military aircraft definitely landed there. In official documents it was referred to as RNAS Larne and subsequently as RAF Larne.

Before the war ended plans had been made to introduce a much larger type of airship, the rigid, Zeppelin-type 33-Class, to patrol out into the Atlantic. Preliminary planning began on a suitable shed near Lough Neagh but the Armistice was signed before this was completed.

By virtue of its geographical situation and in the light of the technology available at the time, Bentra had played a small but vital part in the network of airship stations which had contributed so importantly to winning the first anti-submarine war. No other contemporary aircraft could have performed the jobs the SS and SSZ airships undertook. None could match the airships' endurance or slow speed capability. Their deterrent value was immense - during the entire war there was only one instance of a ship being escorted by an airship being sunk. The submarines were kept below the waves, where they used up valuable battery power and were restricted to a speed of only 8 or 9 knots. A brief log entry from a captured U-boat speaks volumes, "Sighted airship - submerged."

One of General Balbo's Savoia Marchetti S55x flying boats on the waters of Lough Foyle, near Londonderry on 2nd July 1933. (Belfast Telegraph)

The 1920s were a barren time as regards maritime or naval aviation in the Province apart from a few courtesy visits by Supermarine Southampton flying boats from No.480 Coastal Reconnaissance Flight of Coastal Area RAF, which alighted on Belfast Lough and Lough Neagh. On 2nd July 1933, 24 Savoia Marchetti S55x flying boats of the Italian Air Force under the command of General Italo Balbo landed on Lough Foyle en-route to Chicago and the first crossing in formation of the North Atlantic. The following day, the Secretary of State for Air, Lord Londonderry arrived at Aldergrove from London in a Hawker Hart of No.24 Squadron RAF. From there he was conveyed to Lough Neagh, where he boarded a Supermarine Southampton flying boat of No.201 Squadron, in which he flew to Lough Foyle to greet General Balbo.

WORLD WAR TWO

ALDERGROVE - NEAR CRUMLIN, CO ANTRIM

It was not until the late 1930s before aircraft of the Royal Navy would again operate in Ulster. In March 1936, as part of its expansion programme due to the increasing likelihood of another European war, the RAF set up an Armament Training Camp at Aldergrove. Fairly rudimentary target facilities already existed on the eastern shore of Lough Neagh to meet the needs of 502 (Ulster) Bombing Squadron, created in 1925 as a Special Reserve Squadron. These were developed and expanded to provide for practice and live bombing, as well as air to air and air to ground firing. Up to the end of 1939, for periods of two or three weeks at a time, at least thirty-five different units of the RAF visited Aldergrove. Then, in November 1939, 774 Naval Air Squadron (NAS) arrived as part of No.3 Bombing and Gunnery School (which had been developed from the earlier No.2 Armament Training Camp and No.2 Armament Training School) with Fairy Swordfish, Blackburn Roc, Shark and Skua aircraft to provide Telegraphist Air Gunner training. It has the distinction of being the first

Above: Blackburn Roc 774 NAS
(I Henderson Collection)

Left: Blackburn Skua 774 NAS
(Author's Collection)

A Blackburn Roc photographed from a Fairey Swordfish over Portmore Lough in 1940. (E Cromie Collection)

Fleet Air Arm (FAA) squadron to be based in Northern Ireland and remained there until July 1940.

Early in 1940 with the overall war position looking somewhat gloomy and with the RAF's resources considerably overstretched, no fighter aircraft could be spared for the protection of the Province. To cover the gap the Bombing and Gunnery School was reorganised into a fighter squadron with Blackburn Rocs and Skuas, two medium bomber squadrons with Fairey Battles and a reconnaissance squadron with Fairey Swordfish and Blackburn Sharks. This was very much a stop-gap measure but was the first signal of hostile intent from aircraft of the FAA based in the Province.

SYDENHAM - (BELFAST HARBOUR AIRPORT) CO DOWN

The situation of the airport alongside the deep water berth of the Musgrave Channel became particularly important for the loading and unloading of aircraft onto merchant ships and aircraft carriers. To this end, two special wharves were constructed by the Admiralty. The first naval aircraft which have been recorded as using the airfield were the Fairey Fulmar fighters of 803 NAS which arrived in November 1940 prior to their embarkation on the new Belfast-built aircraft carrier HMS *Formidable*.

An attempt to devise a solution to the problem posed to convoys by German long-range Focke-Wulf Condors, was the development of Fighter Catapult Ships (FCS) and Catapult Aircraft Merchant Ships (CAM ships) in 1941. In March 1941 804 NAS was transferred from RNAS Yeovilton to RAF Sydenham under the command of Lieutenant Commander PH Havers

A Fairey Fulmar at Sydenham in 1940. (Author's Collection)

RN. The Squadron's main function was to provide aircraft and air crew to CAM ships to give air defence whilst escorting convoys. The RAF operated a parallel Merchant Ship Fighter Unit (MSFU) from Speke airfield near Liverpool.

The CAM ships originally carried Fulmars which could be launched if a Condor approached a convoy. The aircraft could not land back on the ship again so either had to ditch or head for the nearest friendly territory – Ireland. The first operational launch was from HMS *Pegasus* on 11th January 1941. After chasing away the Condor, the Fulmar, flown by Petty Officer J Shaw made a safe landing at Aldergrove. Subsequently another landed at Sydenham on 7th June, a third sadly crashed into a hillside on 7th July. On 27th August Fulmar N4072 (Sub-Lieutenant Birrell and Leading Naval Airman Sykes) was launched from HMS *Ariguani*. After engaging the enemy Birrell flew for two hours to make a landing at Tramore Strand in Co Donegal. He was able to take off again and made his way to Eglinton.

Hawker Sea Hurricanes were also allocated to the task and were to prove much more effective in the role. HMS *Maplin*, the former Ffyffes banana boat *Erin*, which was based in Belfast, soon became the only such ship manned by FAA pilots and crew. On 3rd April 1941, whilst escorting a convoy homeward bound from Sierra Leone and 450 miles from Lands End, Squadron Senior Pilot, Lieutenant Bob Everett, was catapulted off to attack an approaching Focke-Wolf Condor. (Everett had been a pre-war jockey having won the Grand National in 1929 on the 100/1 outsider Gregalach.) His shooting down of the Condor was the first destruction by any CAM ship pilot of an enemy aircraft attacking a convoy. After the engagement he ditched his Hurricane and was picked up by the convoy escort destroyer HMS *Wanderer*.

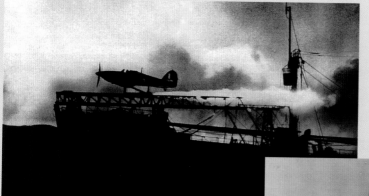

Below: A Hurricane is prepared for launch from a CAM ship (via Mike Lewis)

Above: A Hawker Hurricane is launched from a ship's catapult. (via Mike Lewis)

On 14th September another Squadron pilot, Lieutenant Cecil Walker, destroyed a second Condor after being launched from *Maplin* and subsequently baled out into the sea to be picked up by escort destroyer HMS *Rochester*.

Sub-Lieutenant (A) David Wright RNVR joined 804 in October 1941 as junior pilot under Lieutenant Commander Havers (and later his replacement Major AE 'Minnie' Marsh, Royal Marines) being twice embarked in *Maplin* on convoy protection duty, between which he was based at Sydenham (which changed its name to RAF Belfast in November). While at Sydenham he spent many an evening in the bar of the Grand Central Hotel in Belfast, which was the "in" place at that time. In May 1942, 804 Squadron transferred to Yeovilton in order to prepare for aircraft carrier borne operations in the forthcoming invasion of North Africa. David Wright was left at Sydenham in charge of newly formed 702 NAS, with new pilot recruit Sub-Lieutenant Bill Sturgess, three Hurricanes and a maintenance party of eleven rating technicians, to continue crewing *Maplin* until July 1942, when CAM ship activities ceased in favour of small aircraft carriers, which were becoming available to protect convoys under the American lease/lend agreement.

The increasing number of naval aircraft passing through, Swordfish, Spitfires and Seafires resulted in another change of name. On 21st June 1943, RAF Belfast became RNAS Belfast, HMS *Gadwall*, a shore station of the Fleet Air Arm under C-in-C Western Approaches. As a Royal Naval Air Station the main functions of Sydenham were as an aircraft maintenance and shipment centre, as a base for disembarked squadrons and also for first line Fleet Air Arm squadrons operating on detachment with aircraft carriers in the North Atlantic. Further types included Grumman Wildcats, Martlets, Avengers and Hellcats, Chance Vought Corsairs, Fairey Fireflies and Barracudas. Other non-naval aircraft came for the American forces too, among them Lockheed Lightnings, Republic Thunderbolts and North American Mustangs for the USAAF. Following unloading, the aircraft were test flown and then delivered to maintenance units to bring them up to operational readiness. As the war drew to a close, Sydenham became chiefly an aircraft storage unit but in 1945, work was begun to develop the site as a Royal Naval Aircraft Maintenance Yard for the very specialised task of repairing and reconditioning of naval

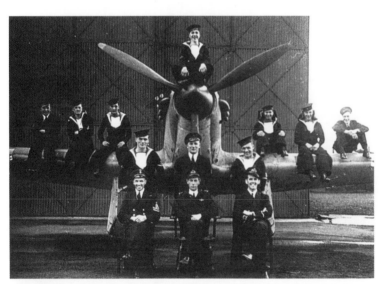

The officers and men of 702 NAS Sydenham 1942. (David Wright)

aircraft. Hangars and workshops were erected on the eastern side of the airfield.

EGLINTON, CO LONDONDERRY

The site was first surveyed by the Air Ministry Airfields Board in July 1940, two months later construction was approved at a cost of £850,000. The Royal Engineers laid the runways over that winter, buildings were constructed and RAF Eglinton opened in April 1941 as a satellite airfield to Limavady. It was intended to be a Coastal Command base. Its first residents were ten Lockheed Hudsons detached from No.53 Squadron. These were followed by the Hawker Hurricanes of No.504 Squadron, as well as a detachment of Boulton Paul Defiants from No.153 Squadron. Londonderry, only a few miles away along the coast of Lough Foyle, was a major naval base of supreme importance to the escort vessels which guarded the Atlantic convoys. Up to 20,000 sailors could be found in port at any one time from the Royal Navy, Royal Canadian Navy, United States Navy, as well as Free French, Polish, Dutch and even Russian. Therefore it was decided that Eglinton would become a day fighter base for the defence of one of the most vital ports in the Battle of the Atlantic. The station was transferred to the control of Fighter Command later in that year. Eglinton's first fighters were the Hurricane IIbs of No.133 (Eagle) Squadron which arrived in the autumn of 1941. (There were three Eagle squadrons - formed from volunteers from the USA who had enlisted in the RAF, either from a sense of adventure or from a desire to get to grips with the Nazis.)

Eglinton at that time had three concrete runways but little else, being described as "a vast sea of mud surrounded by knee-deep lakes of mud and water." Accommodation consisted of nine dispersed sites including sick quarters and communal locations. Maintenance was carried out in two Bellman hangars and 12 blister-type hangars. There were12 bi-pen and 12 small dispersals. Several RAF Spitfire squadrons and, from 1942, the United States Army Air Force (USAAF) also flew from Eglinton. No.134 Squadron RAF reformed there after service in Russia and No.152 Squadron flew convoy patrols for several months in 1942. Eglinton was host to the three squadrons of Spitfires of the 52nd Fighter Group USAAF and the 40 plus Lockheed P-38 Lightnings of the 82nd Fighter Group in 1942, as they trained and worked up for operational deployment. It was the first operational base used by the USAAF in Northern Ireland. In the summer of 1942 the 2nd Fighter Squadron of the 52nd Fighter Group was detached to Maydown, four miles to the west of Eglinton, for a short period. This process was repeated by the 97th Fighter Squadron of the 82nd Fighter Group in October. These squadrons flew the first operational and training missions from Maydown.

On 1st May 1943 Eglinton was loaned to the Royal Navy, along with its satellite airfield at Maydown. Further hangars were erected, ten small Type S plus several of the larger Pentads. The first RN aircraft to arrive were the Fairey Swordfish of 835 and 837 NAS which transferred from Ballykelly on 30th May. They were joined by a detachment from No.275 Squadron RAF, flying Avro Ansons and later the Supermarine Walrus, in the air-sea rescue role. 725 NAS was formed at Eglinton in August 1943 for target towing and other second-line duties, it was equipped with Rocs, Skuas and Miles Martinets. HMS *Gannet*, as it became on 15th May 1943, was used primarily for the working up of RN fighter units - Wildcat,

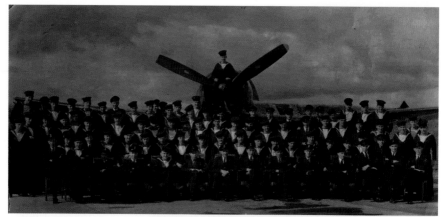

Top: The members of 892 NAS at Eglinton pose with a Hellcat NFII in 1945. (City of Derry Airport)

Right: Hellcat 1 of 1839 NAS Eglinton in 1943. (Mick Burrow)

Below Right: Hellcats at Eglinton in 1944. (Mick Burrow)

Bottom: Batsman gives the 'cut' signal to a Hellcat at Eglinton in 1944. (via Ernie Cromie)

Top: Wildcat V at Eglinton in 1944. (Mick Burrow)

Left: Wildcat VI of 794 NAS at Eglinton in November 1945. (Mick Burrow)

Below Left: Corsair IV KD283 of 1835 NAS on board HMS Premier in the Irish Sea in July 1945. (JD Buchanan via Raymond Burrows Collection)

Bottom: Corsair KS774 of 1851 NAS at Eglinton in January 1945. (Raymond Burrows Collection)

Martlet, Seafire, Hellcat and Corsair. Three Naval Fighter Wings (NFW) were formed there, the 5th, 7th and 10th. Squadrons formed, re-formed and trained prior to embarking either onto large Fleet Aircraft Carriers such as HMS *Indefatigable* or HMS *Glory*, or the smaller Escort Carriers like HMS *Searcher* or HMS *Pursuer*. The Escort Carrier concept was of vital importance in winning the Battle of the Atlantic. These were essentially mass-produced hulls, mostly constructed speedily in US shipyards and fitted with a flight deck, arrester wires and an elastic crash barrier. The first two Grumman F6F Hellcat squadrons to commission for operational FAA service, 800 NAS and 804 NAS, did so from Eglinton in 1943, from whence they proceeded to the escort carrier, HMS *Emperor*, for service on the convoy run to Gibraltar.

MAYDOWN, CO LONDONDERRY

Maydown, which became HMS *Shrike* on 1st January 1944 and had a capacity for 105 aircraft, was the headquarters for MAC-ship (Merchant Aircraft Carrier) operations. This third type of aircraft carrier proved to be a highly effective countermeasure to the U-boat offensive from mid-1943 onwards. These were standard grain carriers or oil tankers fitted with an elementary flight deck, arrester wires and a crash barrier, from which a flight of three or four Swordfish was operated. The MAC-ships were Merchant Navy crewed with a Royal Navy air component; in honour of this fact, on some of the aircraft, the words Royal Navy on the rear fuselage of the white-painted Swordfish were replaced with Merchant Navy. Many of the officers also wore with pride a small, silver Merchant Navy badge in the

Shore maintenance backup team with Swordfish at Maydown in the winter of 1944-45. (Stanley Brand)

lapel of their jackets. They were entitled to do this as in order to come under the jurisdiction of the Master of the ship all RN personnel on board had to sign ship's articles as deckhands for which they were rewarded with a shilling a month (never paid) and a bottle of beer a day (always claimed). The tankers had a longer flight deck but no hangar, the grain ships a small hangar and a lift. Both types could still be used as merchantmen. Each flight of Swordfish flew from Maydown to join its carrier off the Irish coast and returned to base after the journey across the Atlantic and back. It is a remarkable fact that, of the 217 convoys in which a MAC-ship sailed between May 1943 and the end of the war, only one was attacked successfully by a U-boat. Normally two MAC-ships would escort a convoy. Swordfish based on the MAC-ships carried out 4177 patrols and searches, averaging 13 per crossing, of which they accomplished 323. Conditions at Maydown were a little basic, being described as, "a windy little airfield not far from Lough Foyle with a collection of Nissen huts in a sea of mud and a toy-like control tower". Morale was high and much of this was due to

Right: A Swordfish of 836 NAS with underwing rocket projectiles. (Author's Collection)

Above: Swordfish of the Dutch-manned 860 NAS at Maydown. (via Ray Sturtivant)

the charismatic leadership of Lieutenant Commander Ransford Slater RN, 836's CO. The fact that the airfield was reasonably close to the border with the Irish Free State was also regarded as a bonus, as rations were supplemented by a supply of meat and vegetables from neutral territory. Contraband was also brought back from Canada, birdseed surprisingly being a profitable import. Three parent units for the Swordfish were based at Maydown, 836 NAS and 860 NAS for operational deployment and 744 NAS for training. 836 was the largest operational squadron in the FAA. 860 was distinctive in that it was primarily crewed by Dutchmen of the Royal Netherlands Navy. Together the Maydown squadrons provided over 90 Swordfish for some 19 MAC ships. One of 836's pilots, Stanley Brand, later paid tribute the work of the ground crews at Maydown, "The work of our back-up team of skilled and enthusiastic experts, who knew us and were proud of their contribution to what we were doing, gave a feeling of great security and re-assurance, very necessary in an aircraft with a single engine when 1000 miles from land." When a Swordfish returned to Maydown after escorting a convoy it was given, "a sorely needed service, after experiencing all the rigours of a crossing, without a hangar, tied down on deck, exposed to salt water spray, iced up and with compasses (upon which our lives were entirely dependent for accurate air navigation over the ocean) exposed to the magnetic influence of 8000 tons of MAC ship."

The final operational Swordfish flight from a MAC-ship was made on 28th June 1945 from the *Empire Mackay*. The last FAA squadron to relinquish the famous Swordfish was 836 at Maydown in July 1945.

Wrens Joan Feather and Elizabeth Wigg at Maydown in 1945. (Mrs Joan Long)

Joan Feather served as a Wren in the control tower at Maydown in the final months of the war and has vivid memories of watching surrendered U-boats coming up Lough Foyle escorted by Allied warships, as well as naval aircraft from Eglinton and Maydown. They watched from the vantage point of the railway line – until they were moved on as a train was coming. Later they were allowed to visit the submarines, Joan was appalled at the lack of space and the smell. She also recalled the pleasure of cycling between Maydown and Limavady in the beautiful countryside and the popularity of fresh produce from over the Border – eggs, ham, brown bread and butter – some of which she was able to take home to her parents in Yorkshire when going on leave.

Other types serving there before the war's end included the Grumman Avengers of 846, 850 and 856 NAS for relatively brief periods in 1943 and 1944 and the Barracudas of 821

The flying control staff at Maydown in September 1945. (Mrs Joan Long)

NAS for a few weeks in May and June 1945, when it was working up for anti-submarine work in the Indian Ocean/Pacific Theatre. One of the young "Barra" pilots was Sub-Lieutenant David "Jimmy" James RNR, who was on his first visit to Ulster (and who will feature more than once in this story). He had come to Maydown for a two week anti U-boat (AU) course with 744 prior to joining 821. As part of the training he was supposed to experience a trip in a submarine, however time was short and all that could be fitted it was a short descent to the bottom of Belfast Lough - virtually alongside its mooring. The course also included ground school and flying two anti-submarine exercises. The squadron of 16 aircraft then embarked on board HMS *Trumpeter* before sailing to the Far East.

January 1945 saw the arrival in Northern Ireland of a squadron that would be of major importance in the history of Eglinton. The Barracudas of 815 NAS came to RAF Mullaghmore in Co.Londonderry for a brief stay. The Squadron historian was not impressed, "Conditions were extremely primitive (a condition not at all uncommon in that country). On arrival at Mullaghmore one pilot was awarded the MHDOIF (Most Honourable Decoration of the Immovable Finger - as immortalised by Pilot Officer Prune) for mistaking the pundit for a red light and going round again. During the next two weeks of anti-submarine patrols five possible U-boat sightings were reported but no definite results obtained."

A Fairey Barracuda III of 744 NAS at Maydown in 1946. (John Devenney via Raymond Burrows Collection)

LONG KESH, CO DOWN

A number of Fleet Air Arm squadrons were resident at Long Kesh in 1944-45 for Army Co-operation and other training. Types of aircraft included Hellcats, Seafires, Wildcats and Swordfish. At the conclusion of the work-up several squadrons departed Long Kesh for operations at sea on board Escort Carriers. For example the Seafires of 809 NAS embarked on HMS *Stalker* and took part in operations in the Mediterranean, as also did 879 NAS on HMS *Attacker*. On Christmas Eve 1944 the Grumman Wildcat Mk.V, JV482, of 882 NAS took off from Long Kesh but very shortly afterwards had to ditch in Portmore Lough, just east of Lough Neagh. The pilot, Sub-Lieutenant (A) Peter Lock RNVR, managed to reach the shore but his aircraft remained beneath the water for 40 years. It was then recovered and remarkably is now the major restoration project in the Ulster Aviation Society's Heritage collection at the same airfield.

Left: Grumman Wildcat Mk V JV705 of 882 NAS in November 1944.
Right: Sub-Lt (A) Peter Lock. (both Peter Lock via Raymond Burrows Collection)

NUTTS CORNER, CO ANTRIM

Nutts Corner, which commenced operations as a Coastal Command base in 1941, subsequently, in 1943, became a transatlantic terminal and staging point for hundreds of aircraft crossing the ocean. On 8th July 1945 the airfield came under Royal Navy jurisdiction and was commissioned as HMS *Pintail* two days later. It was equipped to handle first line fighter squadrons with a capacity for 60 aircraft but with the end of the war at hand it was used principally for the disbandment of one Hellcat, six Seafire and three Corsair squadrons. It was taken over by No.4 Group Transport Command on 31st March 1946 and then opened as the civil airport for Northern Ireland on 1st December, replacing Belfast Harbour Airport at Sydenham. Nutts Corner then in turn gave way to Aldergrove in October 1963.

Landing accident at Nutts Corner in February 1946 involving a Seafire F.XV of 883 NAS. (G Standley via Ray Sturtivant)

BALLYHALBERT, CO DOWN AND KIRKISTON, CO DOWN

Ballyhalbert was transferred to the Admiralty in on 14th July 1945 and commissioned as HMS *Corncrake*, becoming the home of No.4 Naval Air Fighter School. During the period 1944-45 many naval fighter types passed through or undertook training courses, including Fulmars, Spitfires, Seafires, Hellcats and Corsairs. The 3rd NFW was re-formed there in autumn 1944 and re-equipped with Hellcats. Ballyhalbert's satellite airfield at Kirkiston also became navalised as HMS *Corncrake* II. Ballyhalbert was paid off to care and maintenance on 13th November 1945.

CHAPTER 2

— o○o —

Post-War - Eglinton and Maydown

Following the end of the war in Europe, on 19th July 1945 two silver Dakotas of No.24 Squadron arrived at Eglinton from Long Kesh with King George VI, Queen Elizabeth and Princess Elizabeth on board KN386, which was specially fitted out to VIP standards. The Royal visit was part of the Victory tour of Northern Ireland, which included the opportunity to see 52 surrendered U-boats tied up at Lisahally on the Foyle.

Training units based at Eglinton during the early post-war years for fighter, anti-submarine and strike duties were respectively:

(a) 794 NAS, which arrived in August 1945 from RNAS St Merryn (HMS *Vulture*), equipped with Corsairs, Fireflies, Wildcats, Martinets, Harvards and hooked Spitfire Vbs. The

19th July 1945: the King and Queen visit Eglinton as part of the Victory Tour of Northern Ireland. (FAA Museum)

Right:
The Royal
Dakotas
arrive at
Eglinton.
(FAA
Museum)

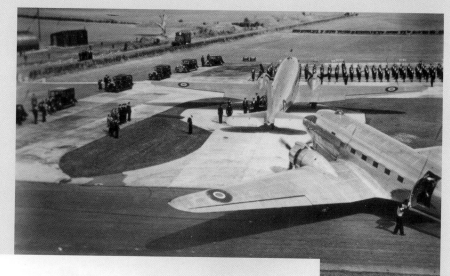

Left: The King,
Queen and Princess
Elizabeth at Eglinton
on 19th July 1945.
(FAA museum)

Squadron was divided into three flights giving instruction in the roles of ground attack, air-to-air combat and photo-reconnaissance.

(b) 744 NAS had re-formed at Maydown 6th March 1944 to provide training for the locally based 836 NAS crews. In October 1945, when it moved to Eglinton it was equipped with Barracuda III aircraft. Ansons were added in August 1946. As well as carrying out training duties they were utilised by the Station Flight.

(c) 719 NAS had originally formed at St Merryn in June 1944 as an air firing training squadron but on 2nd January 1945 had disbanded into 794 NAS. It re-formed again at RNAS Fearn (HMS *Owl*) on 1st March 1946 as a strike training squadron equipped with Barracudas and moved to Eglinton on 14th May 1946 to become part of the newly formed 51st Training Air Group, which was to include a re-formed 718 NAS which provided Seafire conversion courses.

(d) 795 NAS carried out refresher flying to carrier standard on Firefly FR.1s.

Above: 719 NAS in 1946 (Lt Cdr E Meadowcroft via Raymond Burrows Collection)

Right: A crashed Barracuda being examined by one of Eglinton's ground crew. (Don MacGregor)

Above: Two Barracudas of 815 NAS. (Don MacGregor)

A Seafire which made a nose-up landing during ADDLs. (Don MacGregor)

Firefly FR.1 of MB726 203Q of 814 NAS over Eglinton in 1947. (Don MacGregor)

(e) A communications flight of 782 NAS with de Havilland Domines was also stationed there in 1945-46.

Maydown became home to a detachment of 794 NAS, now part of No.3 Naval Air Fighter School in late 1945, for Aerodrome Dummy Deck Landings (ADDLs), on a part of the airfield marked out like an aircraft carrier's deck complete with painted "arrestor wires" and controlled by a batman standing to the starboard side of the "flight deck" threshold with his bats and a portable radio. Lieutenant Jimmy James RN returned to Maydown, now HMS *Gannet* II, in October 1946 with 812 NAS, flying Firefly FR.1s. The squadron had reformed on 1st October and along with the Seafires of 804 NAS, was part of the 14th Carrier Air Group (CAG), which was working up for service in HMS *Theseus*. He recalled that Maydown's CO was a very genial Commander RN, who was a great horse lover. Indeed so great was his affinity with equine life, that he regularly undertook his inspections of the airfield on horseback. Also based there was a sonobuoy tracking school. Flying from Maydown ceased for good in January 1949. It is now an industrial estate but some of the former runway and most of the perimeter track can still be discerned from the air.

In a development that could only but enhance the importance of Eglinton to the region, owing to its proximity to Londonderry, the Joint Anti-Submarine School (JASS) situated at the RN Barracks, Ebrington, HMS *Sea Eagle*, Londonderry opened officially on 30th January 1947. Its task was to run training courses - with the emphasis on combined air and sea tactics - for airmen and sailors. Is was directed and staffed jointly by Naval and RAF officers, with additional input from a US Naval Liaison Officer. It defined its purpose thus, "to get airmen (light and dark blue together) so that each may understand the others' problems and limitations and learn how they can best work together to kill the enemy or render him ineffective. Co-operation is undoubtedly the key to successful anti-submarine (A/S) operations and is a recurring theme at the School." Some measure of the importance placed on constantly improving the standard of A/S warfare and tactics may be gained from reflecting on the fact that out of a total of seven RN fleet and escort carriers sunk by the enemy in World War II, no less than five were victims of torpedoes fired from submarines. The aim was to constantly review and improve the tactics required to combat the ever growing threat posed by the Soviet submarine fleet.

Joint Unit Courses lasted four weeks, places being given to RN, RAF and US Navy squadrons. Naval aircraft operated from Eglinton for the duration, while larger maritime aircraft (heavies) were accommodated at Ballykelly, Aldergrove or in the case of flying boats, Castle Archdale. The course offered the opportunity to drop and monitor sonobuoys on submarines, to bomb them with inert "break-up" weapons, to home ships into their vicinity and to exercise all the associated drills. In addition war games were played by syndicates on large tactical floors - "here the most monumental boobs can be made in perfect safety and no matter the state of the actions, "elevenses" are a must." The School provided a rare chance to operate all the elements of A/S warfare together against live "targets" and possibly even more importantly, to subsequently socialise, get to know and discuss ideas and lessons learned with other specialists. The permanent air element was provided initially by the Barracudas of 744 NAS at Eglinton and the RAF's JASS Flight at Ballykelly, equipped with

A Shackleton from Ballykelly and a submarine taking part in a JASS exercise in the Irish Sea in the early 1950s. (Author's Collection)

Wargaming on the tactical floor at JASS 1953. (Author's Collection)

A Shackleton from Ballykelly over Royal Navy warships on the Foyle. The 3rd Training Squadron, comprising at that time four Loch Class frigates and two C Class destroyers. (Author's Collection)

two Avro Lancaster GR.3s, a Vickers Warwick and an Avro Anson. They were joined in 1948 by the Air Sea Warfare Development Unit (ASWDU), which also flew Lancasters. Aircraft operated with the frigates of the 3rd Training Squadron for exercises, along with other warships and submarines.

Four CAG, the 13th (800 NAS/Seafires, 827 NAS/Fireflies), 15th (802 NAS/Seafires and 814 NAS/Fireflies) and 17th (807 NAS/Sea Furies, 810 NAS/Fireflies) formed at Eglinton in 1946-47. When a young Lieutenant RN, Desmond Cassidi, who grew up in Portglenone in Co Antrim, flew his Firefly FR.1 of 814 NAS from Eglinton to land onboard HMS *Vengeance* as part of 15th CAG in the spring of 1947, it was the first of several visits that this distinguished naval aviator would make. 814 was composed of a high proportion of RNVR officers, so the regulars such as Lieutenant Cassidi tended to be allocated the staff duties, he was duly nominated as Air Group Stores Officer. The time at Eglinton was spent in carrying out ADDLs, formation flying, air firing, observer training and carrier drills. The Rolls-Royce Griffon engined Firefly was a very capable aeroplane but could be tricky to land on a carrier as it had a tendency to float into the barrier or over the side unless due care and attention was observed.

The 15th Carrier Air Group which formed at Eglinton in 1946-47. (Lt Cdr E Meadowcroft via Raymond Burrows Collection)

The 13th CAG had the distinction of being the first CAG to be formed since the Admiralty took the decision to disband all first-line squadrons until peacetime requirements were known. During 800's stay at Eglinton it was intended to give every pilot 50 hours flying with the sole object of teaching the squadron to fly as a "team" – to the exclusion of all other training. After re-equipping with "high-speed" finished Seafire XVIIs in January 1947, the whole CAG embarked on HMS *Triumph* for the Mediterranean. Both squadrons were still on board when the Korean War began on 25th June 1950 – the squadrons making the first attack by RN aircraft on 3rd July.

Top and Bottom: Barracuda IIIs of 815 NAS. (Mick Burrow)

On 9th May 1947 it was confirmed officially that Eglinton had been transferred from the RAF to the RN with effect from 4th March 1947, under the administration of Flag Officer Flying Training, having been on loan since May 1943.

744 NAS was elevated to first-line status becoming the re-formed 815 NAS on 1st December 1947. It was to assume a very significant role in the life of the Station over the next decade and more, being used for many A/S co-operation investigations and exercises with JASS as well as making annual trips to sea to take part in large Fleet and NATO exercises. The first of the latter was on board HMS *Implacable* in May 1948, the last and in fact, the last ever for a Barracuda was in HMS *Indomitable* in May 1951. The Squadron historian waxed lyrical upon its introduction, "The Barracuda, originally intended for the scrap-heap as being an out-dated torpedo and dive-bomber, so equipped, 815 was for a long time the only A/S squadron in the Fleet Air Arm." Be that as it may, it was highly manoeuvrable, surprisingly agile and was a capable dive and torpedo bomber. It gave the FAA good service. The Barracudas were also flown to the aircraft yard at Sydenham from time to time when major overhaul was due. They were frequent visitors until May 1953 on which date 815 NAS re-equipped with eight Grumman Avengers. Many of the Barracudas were scrapped on-site

at Sydenham in August of that year. The yard staff were highly praised by the Squadron for excellent service on a small pool of elderly aircraft. There were sufficient repair facilities at most RNAS to repair damage sustained in heavy landing provided that the airframe had not been stressed; mainplanes, flaps, cowlings, engines, propellers and undrcarriages could usually be attended to on-site. The attrition rate on most training squadrons was quite high, this was reflected in a higher provision for maintenance ratings.

Following the end of World War Two both the Royal Canadian Navy (RCN) and Royal Australian Navy (RAN) were keen to develop naval aviation for themselves. Many Canadians and Australians had served gallantly with the Royal Navy and many subsequently transferred to the new RCN and RAN squadrons along with many "loaned" FAA aircrew,

who availed themselves of the opportunity to emigrate and start a new life overseas. 825 NAS re-formed at Eglinton on 8th August 1947, equipped with Firefly FR.4s, alongside

Above: A Firefly FR.4 of 737 NAS after a heavy landing. (Don MacGregor)

Left: HMCS Magnificent with Fireflies on the foredeck. (USN via www.hazegrey.org)

Right: Sea Furies fly over the Station Mast at Eglinton. (Don MacGregor)

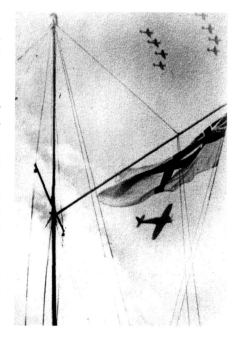

sister squadron 803 NAS with Hawker Sea Fury F.10s. Following working-up both squadrons flew to RNAY Sydenham where they were loaded onto HMCS *Magnificent* in May 1948 and departed for Canada. The unique RN Aerobatic Team, consisting of two Sea Hornets, two Sea Furies and a Sea Vampire, formed at Eglinton before also embarking on HMCS *Magnificent* for a tour of the USA and Canada.

(The first operational RN squadron to form with the Sea Fury, the ultimate piston-engined naval fighter, was 807 NAS, also at Eglinton in 1947.)

Above: HMAS Sydney with Sea Furies lined up on the flight deck. (RAN)

Right: Sea Fury FB.11s of 805 Sqn RAN over Strangford Lough in 1948. (RAN)

Desmond Cassidi returned to Eglinton in May 1948, with the 15th CAG. This was comprised of 802 and 814 NAS, equipped with Sea Furies and Firefly FR.4s respectively. He remembers taking part in air display flying as well as the normal work-up training. This stood the CAG in good stead as along with the 17th CAG in HMS *Theseus*, they sailed to South Africa in HMS *Vengeance*. A highlight of that trip was a sequence of formation flypasts featuring all 48 aircraft of both CAGs at venues around the Union.

As well as Canadians, Australians also availed of Eglinton's facilities with squadrons of Fireflies, 805 NAS, and Sea Furies, 816 NAS, re-forming for transfer to the Royal Australian Navy and embarkation in HMAS *Sydney* in 1948-49. On 15th December 1948, 768 NAS reformed at Eglinton as a Deck Landing Control Officer Training unit with eight Seafire F.15s and two Firefly F.1s. It disbanded three months later having fulfilled its task of producing a batch of 15 DLCOs.

Left: The crew with the Domestic Fire Tender at RNAS Eglinton. (Don MacGregor)

Below: A group photo of the fire appliances at Eglinton, and their crews. (Don MacGregor)

Below: Eddie Parker at the door of the Runway Control Van. (Don MacGregor)

None of the many activities at Eglinton could have taken place safely without the provision of adequate fire and rescue vehicles and equipment. Two of the naval airmen employed there during this period were Eddie Parker and Don MacGregor. They recall that the Fire Station was equipped with a "Monitor" – the standard airfield crash tender, which had an Elahanner Air Foam Pump. This mixed foam compound, air and water to produce a thick substance which had the consistency of toothpaste and which was sprayed from the monitor head to blanket the fire. The water/foam tank had a capacity of 500 gallons. It was crewed by a driver and two rescuers. The driver manned the control unit on the rear and directed the monitor head. The rescue party wore white fearnought suits which had been fireproofed with a mixture of borax and boric acid. Don MacGregor comments, "The main drawback to these fire tenders was that you had to come to a standstill before disengaging the vehicle's road drive and actuating the pump. It also had only two wheel drive which was of little help when in cross-country mode. Moreover, the engine was a very sluggish Ford V8 which gave no acceleration to speak of and almost invariably arrived at the scene of the incident after somebody else had rescued the aircrew and put the fire out!" The "rapid response vehicle" of the time was a converted US Willy's Jeep, which carried two fearnought dressed rescuers, who were equipped with CO_2 extinguishers and a small chemical foam unit. The domestic appliance, or Heavy Mobile Unit, had a crew of six and dealt with non-aviation related fires. It was of a similar standard to a civilian fire engine of that time and as Don remarks, "You did not need any special qualifications to ring the bell!". Don's trade was Naval Airman (Aircraft Handler), he later proceeded to sea to assist with marshalling and controlling aircraft before taking a commission and moving into Air Traffic Control. Eddie Parker was also taken away from fire-fighting duties and while at Eglinton became the driver and operator of a black and white chequered runway control van. His main task was to observe from the port side of the in use runway threshold and contol vehicular and other traffic wishing to cross. He was also responsible for checking that aircraft had their wheels and flaps down for landing, for these duties he was supplied with red and green Very Pistols in the event of radio failure from the van.

A Firefly FR.4 TW749 of Eglinton's 737 NAS crashes into the barrier on HMS Illustrious on 5th October 1949. (Lt Cdr ERA Johnson via Raymond Burrows collection)

In March 1949 737 NAS re-formed to provide Part II of the Operational Flying School Course with Seafires and Fireflies. The Seafires moved on in April 1950, so by the time that Lieutenant Jimmy James was posted to Eglinton again in July 1950 as a Qualified Flying Instructor (QFI) on 737 NAS, it was equipped with the Firefly FR.4 and the Avro Anson and so became the basis for the Naval Anti-Submarine School. This version of the Firefly was fitted with four cannon and could also be armed with rocket projectiles, bombs or mines. However, his stay was not be a long one as he was posted to Korea in the following year. Another officer who was to cross over with Cassidi and James at Eglinton throughout the 1950s was Lieutenant Joe Honywill, who first arrived in March 1951 and stayed for six months. (He had, however, visited Northern Ireland twice during the war, firstly in November 1942, while serving as a Midshipman in the cruiser HMS *Sheffield*. Some 700 US Rangers were embarked in Belfast Lough fresh from their training base at Carrickfergus for the Operation Torch landings in North Africa. Then over Christmas 1943, he was a Sub-Lieutenant in the destroyer HMS *Ulysses*, which had to dock Harland and Wolff's shipyard for repairs.) He had been posted to 815 NAS, which at that time operated the Barracuda III, which was fitted the ASV Mk.X air-to-surface vessel radar housed in a radome under the aft fuselage. Honywill served firstly as a Flight Commander and then as the Senior Pilot. 815 normally carried out mock attacks on submarines with dummy depth charges and smoke bombs, and also undertook work with sonar buoys to give observers practice in tracking submarines. The Barracuda had a crew of three - pilot, observer and telegraphist/air-gunner. Even with a Rolls-Royce Merlin engine, it was rather underpowered for its weight. The extra boost power used for take-off was a necessity rather than a luxury when the aeroplane was fully loaded. Another idiosyncrasy was the configuration of the controls - it was much too easy to progress from selecting flaps to actuating the dive brakes, which if deployed on approach to landing could be a fatal error. Another idiosyncracy was the need to bank to either port or starboard after take-off to relieve the hydraulic pressure on one of the oleos, with the procedure being reversed to get the other leg up and so enable the undercarriage to be raised. These peculiarities were magnified when a pilot converted from the tractable Swordfish. It was often better to proceed to the Barracuda straight from training and learn its ways ab initio. The training regime for the aircraft was itself a little odd as dive bombing came rather too quickly after initial familiarisation in the syllabus.

Another arrival at Eglinton in early 1951 was No.4 Squadron of the Royal Netherlands Navy, with 12 Fireflies, commanded by Lieutenant Commander PJ Leedekerkerken. The Dutch received a warm welcome in Derry but a somewhat hostile response from the Irish Government as reported in the press!

744 NAS re-formed at Eglinton on 20th July 1951 as the Trials and Development Squadron within the recently formed Naval Air Anti-Submarine School and was equipped with Fireflies, Barracudas and Ansons. To begin with it was primarily concerned with the development of search receivers to detect submarine radar. The squadron also acted as the Station Flight with Firefly trainers, Sea Princes and helicopters. In the same month Captain PJ Milner-Barry replaced Captain WT Couchman DSO, OBE, who had been the Station's CO since February 1950, when he had succeeded Captain Sir Aubrey St Clair Ford Bt, DSO, who had been appointed Captain of HMS *Belfast*.

Admiral Sir Rhoderick McGrigor GCB, DSO, the First Sea Lord, with his Flag Lieutenant being met on arrival at RNAS Eglinton in 1951 by Captain PJ Milner–Barry and his Commander (Air), Commander FMA Torrens–Spence DSO, DSC, AFC. (FAA Museum)

By an odd yet happy coincidence, the first report from the Air A/S School in the Fleet Air Arm's magazine *Flight Deck* featured a tongue-in-cheek account of its modernity. At the top of the page was a photograph of "some of the current Observer's Course on an A/S communications sortie" and was in fact an airship of the SSZ type, which had served with the RNAS at Bentra, with a crewman signalling from the nacelle by means of semaphore. The article continued in amusing vein to compare its "top secret" Barracudas and Fireflies "bulging with super priority equipment" with the fighter types "obsolete" Attackers and Meteors - before turning to the serious message of the importance of A/S warfare.

The School now consisted of a Headquarters Staff and three squadrons - 719, 737 and 744. Its main terms of reference were: (a) To provide basic anti-submarine operational training for Pilots (A/S), Observers and Telegraphists (Flying), including initial deck-landing training (DLT) for the pilots. (b) To carry out technical and tactical trials of naval A/S aircraft and their associated equipment as directed by Flag Officer Air (Home). (c) To work in close co-operation with JASS in developing tactics, equipment and training. (d) To carry out refresher training for A/S squadrons already or partially worked up. (e) To run miscellaneous courses in refresher A/S

Supermarine Attacker F.1 WA474 at the Eglinton Open Day in the 1950s. (Hugh McGrattan)

Top: Firefly T.7 WJ167 556GN 719 NAS 1953-54. (Lt Cdr ERA Johnson via Raymond Burrows Collection)

Middle: Firefly T.7s of 719 NAS Eglinton in 1953 during the fleet review at Spithead. (Aviation News)

Bottom: Firefly T.7 WK368 337GN 719 NAS 1953. (Raymond Burrows Collection)

Top: The HQ staff of the Air A/S School at Eglinton in 1953. (Author's Collection)

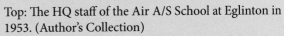

Left: The former CO at Eglinton now Rear Admiral WT Couchman, Flag Officer Flying Training, with a Firefly at Eglinton in 1953. (Author's Collection).

Bottom: A formation of two Fireflies and an Avenger from Eglinton with a Shackleton from 269 Sqn at Ballykelly in 1953. (Author's Collection).

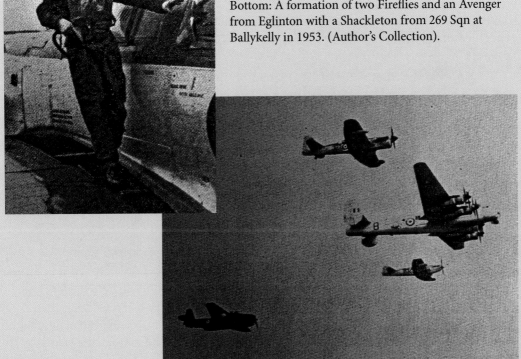

Firefly FR.4 VG 981 of 737 NAS flown by Lt Eric Meadowcroft over Eglinton.
(Lt Cdr E Meadowcroft via Raymond Burrows Collection)

training for pilots and observers, including DLT. The JASS view of the A/S School was, "It is concerned mainly with pipeline training, nuts and bolts and practical mechanics of doing in the air."

737 NAS was the Pilot A/S and DLT Squadron. By 1951 it was equipped with a mix of Fireflies 4 and 5. A staff of eight instructor pilots under the CO, Lieutenant Commander JLW Thompson, conducted the three month course which included general flying, weapon training and crew training by day and night. Ground instruction covered every aspect of A/S warfare with particular emphasis being placed on the joint sea/air aspect of the role. Towards the end of the course the students and their instructors embarked in a training carrier for ten days to qualify in deck-landing (DL) and carrier flying, achieving an average of 20 DLs each. Firefly 6s, which were added to the Squadron by 1953, were used for this phase, these being fully modified with long stroke oleos on the undercarriage legs and hydraulic arrestor hook dampers.

In May 1951 the Squadron was engaged in "Glow Worm" trials. This was a flare head fitted to a three inch rocket projectile (RP). At this date there were four types of RP in use - 25lb armour piercing (tanks and submarines), 60lb HE, 60lb concrete head for range firings and the "Glow Worm". Single aircraft ASW patrols had to carry out their own flare dropping – with parachute flares. These would be dropped just over the radar target and then following a split-S diving turn, attacked from the opposite side to the flares. With "Glow Worm" the attack was made directly on radar and at about three miles (allowing for wind) the nose was pulled up 20 degrees above the horizon, when usually two of the flares were fired. These then illuminated the target after which a straight diving attack was made. When used with the Swordfish, due to the aircraft's slow speed there was usually no chance of overshooting the target. However the Firefly was a different matter. Since the "Glow Worm" was wartime stock some had the rather disturbing habit of having the flare ignite as soon as the RP left the wing, playing havoc with the crew's night vision. Having had this happen on one run, the Squadron's CO left the remainder of the trials to Lieutenant ERA Johnson. Following successful firings on 3rd and 11th May 1951, the final part of the trial was scheduled for 24th off Innishowen with the submarine HMS *Trenchant*. The CO of *Trenchant* was a wartime skipper and although advised to dive as soon as he saw the flares ignite, he chose to remain on the surface, stating that he wouldn't be hit – on the last attack by Firefly 5 VG969, "Johnny" Johnson managed to hit the conning tower with a practice bomb which left a dent in it for all to see.

719 NAS, Lieutenant Commander RHW Blake DSC, was responsible for training Observers and Telegraphists (Flying) and was staffed with 15 pilots. It was equipped with the Firefly T.7, which was a three-seat aircraft of similar configuration to the keenly anticipated Fairey Gannet. This mark of the Firefly was praised by the Squadron as, "a pleasant aircraft to fly, both by day and night, possessing good slow speed handling characteristics, good instrumentation and an excellent view." The flying task was intensive within the six week period allowed, to give the students as much experience as possible of working with ships and submarines.

744 NAS, Lieutenant Commander FE Cowan, continued with its valuable service performing trials on new A/S equipment and liaising closely with front and second line squadrons, to ensure that the trials and tactics were kept on a realistic basis. The Headquarters Staff allocated priorities in the use of ranges, submarines and exercise areas in respect of A/S School aircraft, the Avengers of 815 Tactical A/S Squadron (the last Barracuda having been

A Grumman Avenger AS.5 XB 303 of 814 NAS in 1954-55. It later ditched on 24 August 1955. (Raymond Burrows Collection)

replaced in May 1953) and visiting RN and RNVR squadrons engaged in basic or continuity A/S training. The Chief A/S Instructor in 1953 was Lieutenant Commander PC Heath. He was responsible to the Station's Commander (Air), Commander JG Baldwin DSC, for the organisation, execution and co-ordination of all training, both air and ground.

Until the early 1950s safety duties/search and rescue with regard to aircraft landing in the sea were performed by a Supermarine Sea Otter amphibian. It was replaced by rotary-wing aircraft. The first helicopter to be based at Eglinton may have been the Sikorsky R6 Hoverfly II KN843 of the Station Flight in 1951-52. The R6 was an improved version of the first helicopter in British military service, the Hoverfly R4B. It had a more streamlined appearance and had a more powerful engine but still required quite a degree of physical strength to fly and counteract the rotor pitch imbalance. It flew straight and level at speed with a somewhat rolling motion. It was also prone to engine unreliability due to seepage of oil into the magneto. However the Hoverflys did at least give the three services some initial

Sea Otter RD874 at RNAMY Belfast 1952 (Raymond Burrows Collection)

experience of rotary-wing aviation. It is possible, however, that the Hoverfly's purpose at Eglinton was as a static instructional airframe only, to prepare maintainers for the task of servicing helicopters. It is believed that a Hoverfly 1 (or R4B) first appeared in Irish skies in November 1948. A pair of these from 705 NAS assisted in a hydrographic survey of the Irish coast. A helicopter was based for a time at an Irish Air Corps airfield, Gormanston in Co. Meath. One of the pilots may have been 705's CO, Lieutenant (A) Ken Reed, who later became a test pilot with Westlands. One of the machines came to grief on 21st February 1950, when FT837, flown by Lieutenant Worrall, crashed in the churchyard of the Church of Ireland at Youghal, Co.Cork, following tail rotor failure - the helicopter was seen by eyewitnesses to be spinning around in the air as it came down.

A Dragonfly HR.1, VX600, of the same squadron, flown by Lieutenant Dick Beechener, carried out further aerial surveys between 9th April and 17th October 1951. He flew from Anthorn, near Carlisle, to Aldergrove, escorted by a Firefly. A brief visit was then made to Sydenham for customs clearance before flying across the border to Finner Camp, an Irish Army Base between Ballyshannon and Bundoran in Co Donegal. The helicopter had no RN markings and all personnel connected with the operation, of whom there were about a

Left: Dick Beechner also had considerable experience of flying the Hoverfly, in this case landing on the LST HMS Suvla in 1949. (Dick Beechener)

Middle and Left: Before and after: the Hoverfly which crashed at Youghal in 1951. (both via Eddie Murray)

dozen at Finner, wore civilian clothes. The Officer-in-Charge was Major B Armstrong RE, who was a scratch golfer and was delighted to find that the professional at Bundoran was the renowned Irish golfer, Christy O'Connor. Over the next seven months Dick Beechener flew a total of 55 hours and 20 minutes – comprising 41 survey sorties, air tests and trips to Eglinton for maintenance and spares. The area covered included Ballina and Sligo to the west, Killybegs, Letterkenny and Malin Head to the north. On board there was normally a photographer and an Irish Army officer. Very often the flight would would be out to sea for a few miles, then hovering while a 180 degree panorama of the coast would be taken. The purpose of Operation Sandstone was very secret at the time and covered the whole of the British Isles, surveying ports, coasts, inlets and rivers. In October Beechener was replaced by Lieutenant J Morton. He spent the next few months at Eglinton as an assistant to Commander (Air). The form of transport provided was a motorbike but he still managed to get 20 hours or so flying the Firefly. Beechener later became a pilot with Aer Lingus.

The Sea Otter at Eglinton was replaced by Westland Dragonfly HR.3 and HR.5 from 1952 to 1959. The Dragonfly was the first British-built helicopter to serve with the Fleet Air Arm. It was manufactured under licence from the basic US Sikorsky S-51 design, with many detail changes, the most fundamental of which being the engine, an Alvis Leonides of 550hp. The HR.3 also had all-metal rotor blades which were an improvement on the wooden-ribbed, fabric-covered blades of earlier models. The first Dragonfly to be based at Eglinton was WG724 and was flown in by Lieutenant Harry Morley on 13th December 1952. The flight from Gosport was made in a series of stages and took six hours and thirty-five minutes flying

Above: Dragonfly WG722 918 GN being flown by Tony Wilson. (Tony Wilson)

Left: Dragonfly WH 991 917 GN. (Lt Cdr E Meadowcroft via Raymond Burrows Collection)

time. Having been given the wind direction and the runway in use by ATC, "I duly flew down the runway and round the perimeter track at a height of about six feet and landed in the visiting aircraft park." He was attached to 744 and was joined by Aircrewman Carpenter three days later. As the officer, Harry Morley was allocated a motorbike (possibly the same one ridden by Dick Beechener) to use as transport from the Wardroom to the aircraft in case of emergency. Carpenter and Aircraft Artificer 3 Rittey, the third member of the team, presumably had to walk (or run). Winching training was carried out and good relations were developed with the crews of the Avro Shackletons which were based at Ballykelly from

A Dragonfly from Eglinton overflies 240 Sqn Shackleton MR.1 WB 858 at Ballykelly in 1953. (David Hill)

1952 onwards. Harry Morley assisted with mail runs to ships working out of Derry and various other miscellaneous flying duties. The helicopters were also called upon for tasks in aid of the civil community, not only in Northern Ireland but in the Irish Republic as well. A young girl suffering from acute appendicitis was transported from Tory Island off the coast of Donegal to Eglinton and from there to hospital in Londonderry, where a successful operation was carried out. Shortly after this incident three men stranded by the weather in a lighthouse off the Sligo coast were removed to the mainland at the request of the Irish Lights Commissioners. It was noted that questions were asked in the Dail (the Irish Parliament in Dublin) as to why it was always necessary to contact Eglinton for help whenever a helicopter was required in Eire. (The Irish Air Corps had to wait until November 1963 before receiving its first Alouette III helicopters.)

In 1953, Joe Honywill returned to Eglinton. He had been promoted to Lieutenant Commander and had been appointed CO of 737. By this time the squadron flew Firefly AS.5s and later AS.6s, which were specifically equipped for anti-submarine warfare. The four

DH 89A Dominie NF861 900GN of 744 NAS which crashed near Cushendun in March 1953. (David Hill)

Hispano cannon of previous versions were deleted and provision made for sonobuoys and associated receivers for the detection of submarines. The squadron's task was the final stage of the pilots' course - operational and weapons training, ADDLs at Limavady and carrier landing practice. The Firefly was a very effective aircraft in a range of roles, fleet fighter, anti-submarine and ground attack with solid rockets. One of Honywill's "pupils" was Desmond Cassidi when he returned for a short familiarisation course after a non-flying posting. In January 1954 Jimmy James joined 737, firstly as the 2nd QFI and then as the Senior QFI. One of his least favourite duties at that time was evaluating the students in spins and torque stalls twice each way . After a day putting six to eight trainees through their paces on these manoeuvres he would admit to feeling "very tired". The students, if successful, would soon progress to carrying out their first solo deck landings, at this particular time on board HMS *Illustrious*.

Also in 1953, 706 NAS arrived at Sydenham in Belfast with eight American-built Whirlwind HAS.22s and two Hiller HT.1s. These helicopters were concerned with trials in respect of sonar equipment. They remained in Belfast until October when they embarked in HMS *Perseus*.

In November 1954 Eglinton received the following signal from Flag Officer Flying Training:

> "It is fitting that the last Squadron to be entrusted with the task of taking pupils to a Barriered Deck should have been 737 Squadron, who have done so much in the past to uphold and improve our Deck Landing standards, and I should like to take this opportunity of congratulating all concerned on their magnificent record."

The signal referred to the advent of the angled flight deck on board aircraft carriers which rendered the need for the steel wire barrier obsolete, except in extreme emergencies.

The newly completed HMS Centaur in Belfast Lough in 1953. (Belfast Telegraph)

The barrier limited the use of the entire length of the flight deck as it effectively cut it in two, the fore part was devoted to stowing and launching and the after part to landing only. As heavier and faster jet-powered aircraft were introduced in the 1950s this was no longer a practical proposition. The angled flight deck, which was invented by Captain DRF Campbell, was first experimented with on the light fleet carrier HMS *Triumph* in 1951-52 by means of a white line painted on the flight deck. The first aircraft carrier to be completed with a "half angled" flight deck was the Belfast-built HMS *Centaur*, in September 1953. Aircraft landing on would now approach at an angle to the fore and aft line of the flight deck unimpeded by parked aircraft in front of them; any not catching the arrestor-wire could take off again and have another approach - fuel permitting. The first carrier with a fully angled flight deck was HMS *Victorious*, in 1958, after her extensive rebuild. Landing was also greatly aided by another innovation, which entered service in 1954, the mirror landing-sight, which was developed by Commander (E) HCN Goodhart. A third major contribution to effective carrier operations was the steam catapult, which also entered service in 1954, conceived by Commander CC Mitchell, which combined with the angled deck enabled flying-off and landing-on to take place simultaneously.

Also in 1954, a twenty year old aircraft electrical mechanic, David "Mick" Morrissey, was drafted to Eglinton. He travelled to Stranraer to catch the early morning ferry to Larne - the *Princess Margaret*, a sister ship of the ill-fated *Princess Victoria*, which had sunk in February 1953 with the loss of 128 lives including ratings from Eglinton making a similar journey. The next stage of the trip was by train to Belfast where he changed for Londonderry, being picked up by a Bedford 3-tonner for the final few miles. Eglinton was considered to be one of the best drafts for ratings in the Fleet Air Arm - chiefly because civvies could be worn when going ashore. It should be mentioned at this stage that leaving base, even from a naval shore station, was "going ashore." The wearing of civilian clothing was a sensible precaution. There was a low level of IRA activity, which would develop into the "Border Campaign"

Wardroom games at Eglinton. (Lt Cdr ERA Johnson via Raymond Burrows Collection)

of 1956-62. Security at Eglinton in 1954 was fairly relaxed - the WRNS site was guarded day and night (probably not against the IRA), as was the radio station at Killylane and an area round the armoury was fenced off with barbed wire, floodlights and trip wires. The aircraft dispersals were guarded at night by ratings armed with batons. A roving patrol had .303 rifles but no ammunition. The junior ratings accommodation was spread over three sites with pathways leading to the dining hall, Chiefs' and POs' messes, Wardroom, NAAFI, gym and cinema (two shows a night except Saturdays), barber's shop, CH Bernards naval tailor's shop, stores and guardroom. The author has been told by a reliable source, who wishes to remain anonymous, that the naming of the WRNS site was not without a degree of controversy and indeed embarrassment, when it was discovered that it was to be named, as was the usual practice, after a famous Admiral. The original choice of Effingham was quickly changed to Benbow. The main entrance was about half a mile away, where there was another guardroom as well as the main administrative buildings. The sick bay was across the road from the church in the village.

Morrissey had been drafted to the Station Flight, which had Fireflies, an Avenger, a Hunting Sea Prince communications aircraft and a Westland Dragonfly helicopter. His main job was daily and monthly inspections. He was also responsible for routine jobs on visiting aircraft. Other types visiting the station, working up or being used for training and trials included Grumman Avengers, the Douglas Skyraider AEW 1, the rare Blackburn Firebrand and the even lessed spotted Blackburn YB1, WB797. In passing it may be noted that Joe Honywill had a difficult experience with a Firebrand in 1949. He hit the carrier's "island"

Right: A lineup of visiting Firebrands at Eglinton. (Don MacGregor)

Below: Firebrand TF.5 EK831 of 813 NAS at Eglinton in 1948. (Tony Hughes)

when landing on HMS *Implacable*. It had 18 feet of nose, filled with 300 gallons of fuel, in front of the cockpit. It also had pneumatic controls with a built in time-lag. It was not an easy or forgiving beast, Joe's incident was very far from being unique.

At this time the Station Commander was Captain TWB Shaw DSC. Terence Shaw was an Observer who flew in the daring attack on the Italian Fleet at Taranto on 11th November 1940. He too was a horseman, he rode his bay mare as a home to duty transport and around the Station as appropriate. He was followed in 1955 by Captain John Roe but not on horseback.

Captain TWB Shaw DSC, the Commanding Officer of RNAS Eglinton making his rounds on horseback. (Author's Collection)

CHAPTER 3

— ∘O∘ —

ENTER THE GANNET

Meanwhile at RNAS Ford in Sussex, Lieutenant Commander Cassidi was engaged on work which would have a definitive bearing on the future course of events at Eglinton. As part of X Flight of 703 NAS he was flying an intensive trials programme aimed at bringing an important new naval aircraft into service, this was the Fairey Gannet. Four aircraft and four crews flew the aircraft for 100 hours simulating all parts of the operational envelope. The engine would then be changed and the process start again. Hot weather trials were carried out at Khartoum and deck landings made on HMS *Albion*. On 16th February 1955 Cassidi flew the Gannet T.2, XA508, to Eglinton to begin the conversion and familiarisation process. One of the first pilots whom he checked out was Jimmy James.

Only the month before, still at Eglinton, Joe Honywill had moved from 737 to become CO of 824 NAS, flying the Grumman Avenger AS.4. The squadron was soon to convert to the Gannet but the Avenger was still an impressive machine. Under the Mutual Defence Assistance Program, Britain had received 100 standard

Top and Bottom: The last Fireflies leave Eglinton and escort an incoming Gannet before they depart. (Lt Cdr ERA Johnson via Raymond Burrows Collection)

TBM-3Es from the USA as a stopgap until the Gannet was ready for service. Conversion work undertaken by Scottish Aviation at Prestwick equipped them to British standards as AS.4s and AS.5s. Honywill described it as, "a big tub of an aeroplane with lots of room, plenty of power and a huge bomb bay." One particular incident which happened during that transition period stands out. The squadron crewroom was located on the north-western, Lough Foyle side of the airfield. It was not the most draught-proof of buildings and was heated by a venerable "Smokey Joe" stove. Honywill stood with his back to this welcome heat source and began his customary briefing. He began to notice that the assembled crews were taking less than proper notice of their CO's words of wisdom. He also started to feel quite hot. It was then that he realised that his officers had been distracted by the sight of his trousers gradually emitting steam, then smoke as they started to combust. He also recalled a singular report from a police constable one evening. It was necessary to patrol runway 09/27 as a public footpath ran across it. The policeman contacted Air Traffic to report the following, "A pedestrian on a bicycle is crossing the runway and would not stop."

On 26th April 1955 the Squadron celebrated 21 years of service with a "Coming of Age" party for past and present members. Representatives of the press were also invited to attend. The event was almost upstaged on 24th when the IRA decided to pay a nocturnal visit to the Station. The newspapers duly reported, "after engaging in a spirited gun battle with the sentries, the gunmen made off through the maze of narrow, winding streets and effected their escape without casualties on either side." On the morning of the 26th the visitors were shown over the Squadron dispersal, this was followed in the afternoon by a flying display. After individual exhibitions of slow and high-speed flight by the CO and Lieutenant McGrail, the entire squadron formed up to permit air-to-air photographs to be taken of all the aircraft in formation. The highlight of the party held that evening was the cutting of the birthday cake by the CO's wife, Mrs Dorothea "Dorfie" Honywill. The cake had been made by the Chief Cook of HMS *Gannet* and was complete with battle honours and a model of the Gannet AS.1.

Joe Honywill was most impressed by the Gannet, it seemed a really well-designed, modern aircraft in 1955. The Armstrong Siddeley Double Mamba engine with its twin, co-axial, contra-rotating propellers gave power to spare, especially when flying at low level - a comforting thought when making a long attack run over the sea. Moreover, either half of the coupled power unit could be shut down in flight giving a much extended range. The bomb bay was reputed to be big enough to hold everything but the kitchen sink - a fact which was disproved over Gibraltar one day when a redundant sink was

Mrs JD Honywill cutting 824's 21st Anniversary cake. (JD Honywill)

unloaded for the entertainment of the reviewing Admiral. The Gannet combined the roles of hunter and killer with its ASV radar and its substantial load of torpedoes, bombs, sonobuoys, mines or depth charges. It did have its faults, however, as Lieutenant Commander GWH Gatis, the Senior Observer of 815 wrote in his weekly bulletin in July 1956, "In the submarine exercises we had one submarine to our credit and the discovery that a three and a half hour trip can provide a very adequate local anaesthetic for certain parts of the anatomy of aircrew."

From 1955 onwards Eglinton became especially associated with the Fairey Gannet AS.1s and T.2s of 719 NAS and 737 NAS. Additionally the Gannets of 812, 815, 820, 824 and 847 NAS formed at Eglinton in 1955 and 1956 before embarking on the carriers HMS *Eagle*, HMS *Ark Royal*, HMS *Centaur* and HMS *Bulwark*, or in the case of the last named, Cyprus for land based duties. It may be an apocryphal story but three distinguished retired officers avow that

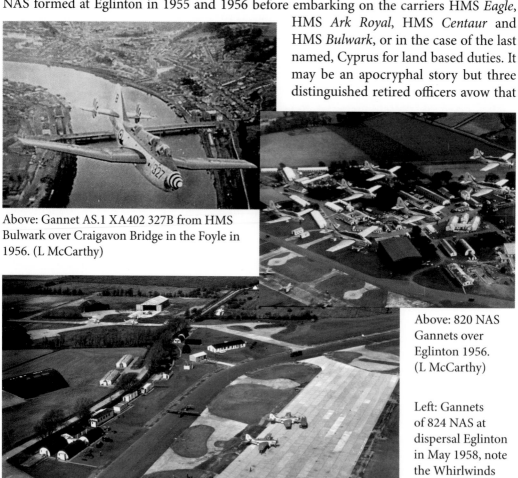

Above: Gannet AS.1 XA402 327B from HMS Bulwark over Craigavon Bridge in the Foyle in 1956. (L McCarthy)

Above: 820 NAS Gannets over Eglinton 1956. (L McCarthy)

Left: Gannets of 824 NAS at dispersal Eglinton in May 1958, note the Whirlwinds in the top left of the picture. (FAA Museum)

embarkation by way of Bangor, Co.Down always seemed to be organised for 12th July when the roads and streets could be guaranteed to be full of marching Orangemen and bands.

Lieutenant Commander Desmond Cassidi assumed command of 820 in the spring of 1955. Lieutenant Commander Joe Honywill was the "Boss" of 824 and Jimmy James was in 737. A friendly rivalry existed between the units but with a competitive edge. 820 acquired the nickname of the Spangles, because of the aeroplanes' purple and white spinners and benefited from the unofficial sponsorship of the makers of the eponymous sweets, a well-known firm in Slough. They recalled that flying from Eglinton was not without interest due to the proximity of a small hill adjacent to the airfield, "quite a hazard for a 300 ft circuit - once aircraft had some radar it was usually possible in bad weather to descend over the sea and with radar detect the entrance to Lough Foyle and come in over the flat sands of Magilligan strand, where the bombing range was located." Benevenagh which rejoiced in the nickname of "Ben Twitch", five miles north-east of Ballykelly was a particular danger to airmen, as it was very close to the airfield approach flight path. Flying in the vicinity of Londonderry was restricted by the location of a mink farm close to Lough Foyle and the city. This necessitated keeping to a minimum height of 1000 feet when in the general area.

Sadly in May 1955, WN427, a Gannet from 820 was lost in the Atlantic 200 miles west of the Scottish coast. After an extensive search, some three hours later, the life raft was found but only one crew member survived, Lieutenant CD Putler. Lieutenant WGW Mulholland and Leading Telegraphist (A) M Forbes had died from exposure.

In another incident that year WN414 was at 300 feet on a radar homing exercise with HMS *Carisbrook Castle*, when a loud bang was heard by the crew. The aircraft ditched but this time all three crew members, Lieutenant DSJ Mosley, Sub-Lieutenant BH Wilkins and Leading Telegraphist (A) WA Jarvis were rescued.

After only a fairly short time with 820, Cassidi was selected for a very interesting posting. He had to learn how to fly the Whirlwind helicopter for a tour with the new ice patrol ship HMS *Protector*. He returned to Eglinton twice more in 1956 and 1958 for Gannet refresher courses.

Lieutenant "Jimmy" James moved to 815 (now commanded by Lieutenant Commander JP David) as Senior Pilot in January 1956, flying the Gannet AS.1. It was equipped with eight of these and a single T.2. The squadron's tail emblem was a harp. This happy co-incidence with the trademark of a brand of stout resulted in a flight for the representatives of Guinness and the provision of a regular supply of barrels of the brew for ratings' parties. The officers were not eligible for the liquid refreshment but could receive branded waistcoat buttons and toucan table lamps. Indeed a Squadron history noted that 815's motto "Strike Deep" was sometimes replaced by "Drink Deep" as a tribute to the brew. (A fondness for the black stuff had already been proven as long ago as 1946 at Maydown by the reputed fact that some 1500 bottles had been consumed at a particularly lively weekend station party, when James was serving with 812). Eglinton was renowned for its conviviality. Joe Knox's pub just outside the main gate was a favourite spot on Saturday from noon onwards. It was a modest double fronted building, the only clue to whose real nature was a small Guinness sign fixed to the wall on one side of the front door. Benches around the walls and a few tables and chairs were

Gannet overflying Eglinton. Joe Knox's pub is at the bottom left of the picture. (D James)

the furnishings common to both front rooms. While officers stayed mainly in one of these rooms and ratings in the other, there was no rigid division. Naval personnel mingled freely with the locals and on many an evening a fiddler or an accordion player would accompany a rousing sing song. It became known as No.9 Issue Centre (the other eight bone fide official stores were on base) and was noted as such in the station telephone list, in order that the urgent command could be relayed "Report for duty from Issue Centre No.9!". The Station Commander in 1956 was Captain TGC Jameson of the whiskey dynasty, which probably did no harm with regard to contacts in the distilling and brewing industries. Certainly the quality of the whiskey at his parties is fondly remembered. At that time the Chief Instructor of the A/S School was Lieutenant Commander CJR Coxon, who was followed in the summer of 1956 by Lieutenant Commander OGW Hutchinson. 737 NAS was commanded by Lieutenant Commander DW Pennick, who noted that all his five instructors were jet converted, " to enable them to appreciate the problems of pilots converting to the turbo-prop Gannet directly from the jet-propelled Vampire". There had been some concern following the introduction of the Gannet that the difference in size as compared to the diminutive Vampire and the profusion of levers in the Gannet's cockpit would cause difficulties for the student pilot. In fact the CO was able to report, " it is generally true to say that the average Provost and Vampire trained pupil from Valley takes the conversion in his stride, perhaps even better than his more senior, but piston-trained counterpart." By this time 737 provided 50 hours flying conversion and A/S training over 10 weeks. This enabled the successful pilots to progress to a front line squadron working up under the air group cycle. The provision of a simulator was keenly awaited.

719's CO was Lieutenant Commander ERA Johnson. Observers undertook a seven week course, while Telegraphists (Air) were trained for four weeks. The keen anticipation here was for the full replacement of the 13 Firefly T.7s by Gannets. IRA activity had increased a little with the result that more barbed wire entanglements had been erected and the Royal Marines detachment had participated in a wider variety of exercises and "emergencies" during the course of Flag Officer Flying Training's (FOFT) annual inspections. Other effects of terrorist activities in the general area were the disruption of power supplies from time to time and an increase to the Station's complement to allow for the provision more guards for the main and outlying sites.

Lt Cdr DW Pennick the CO of 737 NAS with Gannet T.2 XA508. (AgustaWestland)

In April 1956 745 NAS was reformed at Eglinton, under Lieutenant Commander MF Bowen, with four Avenger TS.4s specifically as a trials unit for radar jamming equipment. It was noted that "fitted with new black boxes" it had been doing sterling work in co-operation with HMS *Sea Eagle* and had great success in the Londonderry Joint Exercises.

In August 1956 Telegraphist (Air) Lawrie McCarthy joined 719 to begin an anti-submarine course on the Gannet AS.1. The normal daily routine began with a met briefing at 08.30, followed by either classroom work, day and night flying, with spells in the simulator for submarine location and tracking. When the course concluded after four weeks he joined 820, for "working up" to become part of HMS *Bulwark*'s Air Group. Training comprised navigation, both using dead reckoning and radar, depth charge and torpedo dropping, dive bombing on the Minerney range, submarine chasing and simulated mine dropping. Due to the number of severe gales towards the end of the year, the Gannets carried out a large number of SAR missions looking for fishing boats that had gone missing. Sadly several were found battered and wrecked upon rocky shores. 820 also had a non-fatal mishap during the course of a visit to Belfast by HMS *Bulwark* in early July 1957. The Gannet AS.1 322 was carrying out a catapult launch while the ship was at anchor in Bangor Bay. The hold back broke at the critical moment so the aircraft had to attempt to carry out a free take-off with no more than 100 feet of deck length available. The aeroplane failed to take-off and ditched.

The Gannet AS.1 322 XA 390 from HMS Bulwark being retrieved
from Bangor Bay in July 1957. (Raymond Burrows Collection)

The crew were rescued from the water by excited holidaymakers who had been clustering
around the ship in an assortment of small boats. The aircraft was recovered a week later by
a salvage vessel but it was a complete write-off.

McCarthy also recalled a particular incident which happened when a quarterly wet
dinghy drill was being carried out in Lough Foyle. A Torpedo Recovery Vessel took the ten
participants out from Derry onto the lough. They jumped into the less than inviting waters
and inflated their Mae Wests and dinghy, before tumbling into the latter and awaiting the
arrival of the "rescue" helicopter. Once in the dinghy it was quite pleasant as it was a bright,
sunny and perfectly calm Saturday afternoon. The Dragonfly duly clattered into view and
the winch was lowered. At this time there were a number of German students at Eglinton,
as the West German Navy had purchased 15 Gannet AS.4s and one T.5 trainer. One of the
students was built on very generous lines and as the winch strained to lift him, it became
obvious the helicopter was coming down to meet the "survivor" rather than winched person
going upwards. In these circumstances all the pilot could do was to order the crewman to
cut the winch wire. The German tumbled downwards rapidly, sustaining a large bump on
the head following contact with the cable weight but no other damage. The pilot had made
correct decision and later blamed a combination of the lack of wind (which reduced his
available lift) and the weight on the end of the line.

Another Saturday morning brought another incident which could have had fatal
consequences. The Gannets were carrying out ADDLs when XG875, an aircraft from 737,
approached too low on finals, clipping the embankment of the Belfast to Londonderry railway
line, knocking his nose wheel into the bomb bay and losing a main wheel altogether. The
Gannet staggered back into the air and went around the circuit again. All radio contact had
been lost, so Lawrie McCarthy's aircraft was instructed to fly alongside the stricken machine

and convey a message by hand signals, not to ditch but to do a wheels up landing on the runway. This was achieved successfully despite a near miss with a train. In another incident XA320 of 812 crashed into Lough Foyle while on a night bombing exercise. The aircraft broke up on hitting the water. Luckily, the crew - Lieutenant IML Banyard, Lieutenant JH Merison and Telegraphist (F) DE Woodhead - all survived.

The Gannet Simulator at RNAS Eglinton in 1957. (Author's Collection)

The Gannet Flight Simulator, built by Redifon Ltd., was accepted for Naval service on 1st January 1957, having taken almost two years to complete. It was housed in a separate building with its own air conditioning plant, workshop and office, adjoining the rooms which housed the massed racks of the computer equipment and the simulator itself - which was the front section of a Gannet AS.1. This had all the normal cockpit components installed, connected to an electro-hydraulic assembly which provided feel and control loading throughout the speed range. A very comprehensive simulation was controlled from the adjacent instructor's console, "noise, for instance, ranges from cartridge starting, engine and aero-dynamic noise, down to tyre squeal and taxi rumble on landing." All prospective pilots undertook the Double Mamba Handling Course, whether they were straight from flying training or were experienced pilots undergoing a conversion course. The students progressed from starting the engine and cockpit familiarisation, to general handling, stalling, accidents and emergencies, an "alarming number" of which could be introduced by the instructor. The final stage brought the pupil up to instrument rating standard. Another important part of the training offered was for maintenance personnel, to bring them up to the required standard for ground running the aircraft.

From April until November 1957 flying at Eglinton was suspended and activities were removed to RAF Ballykelly, eight miles to the east, while the runways and taxitracks were repaired. During the following few months a new lighting system was installed and resurfacing work was carried out. As the airfield accommodation at Ballykelly was limited it was not possible to transfer all the aircraft. As a result major servicing was still carried out at Eglinton. The sight of a Gannet being towed along the road between the two air stations was not uncommon. One hangar was allocated for naval use by the RAF and a disused small runway was partially resurfaced to act as an aircraft parking area. Temporary hutted accommodation was provided for officers and crewrooms. The operations and communications staff remained at Eglinton but air traffic control moved to Ballykelly, sharing two caravans in the absence of a control tower, which was undergoing a major refit. A contemporary account described the scene,

A plan of the airfield in the 1950s and a map showing its geographical location. (Author's Collection)

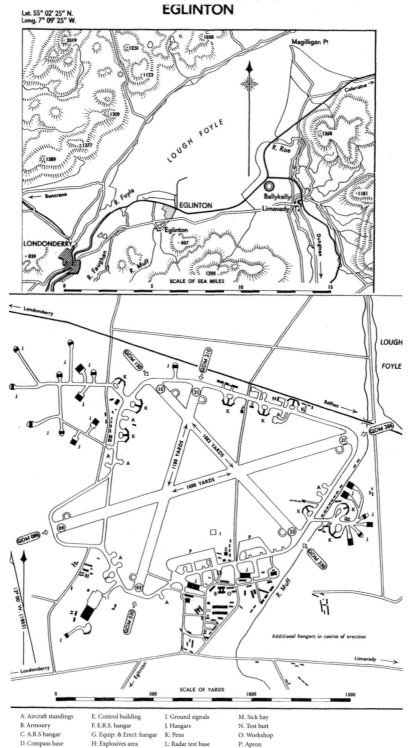

A. Aircraft standings	E. Control building	I. Ground signals	M. Sick bay
B. Armoury	F. E.R.S. hangar	J. Hangars	N. Test butt
C. A.R.S hangar	G. Equip: & Erect: hangar	K: Pens	O: Workshop
D. Compass base	H. Explosives area	L: Radar test base	P: Apron

"Eglinton has now become a maze of trenches consequent upon the complete re-laying of the airfield lighting. The installation of the approach lighting to Runway 27 is awaited with interest, as anyone who knows the vast expanse of extremely glutinous mud which exists on the approach to this runway will readily appreciate."

Many of the features of undergoing training at Eglinton as a typical RN pilot have been recalled by Tony Wilson. Following the completion of his Advanced Flying Training, on Vampires at RAF Valley "and sporting a brand new set of pilot's wings on my sleeve", Midshipman Tony Wilson was posted to 737 NAS as one of seven members of 60 Course to convert to the Gannet and undertake Operational Flying Training (OFT) in anti-submarine warfare. In late June 1957 he began the journey north by way of steam train from Euston station in London to the overnight ferry crossing from Heysham in Lancashire to Belfast. The next part of the trip was by rail again on the line to Londonderry, crossing the runway at Ballykelly (trains had priority except in emergency conditions when ATC had overriding control) and stopping at "the little Eglinton station, rarely used, usually only by special request or when a special train was laid on to take servicemen off to Belfast on the main leave periods." He was reasonably impressed by the accommodation and mess buildings, which were on the other side of the Londonderry to Coleraine road from the airfield. The long huts were of the wartime pre-fabricated, concrete type but the individual "cabins" for officers were centrally heated. His first impression of the Gannet was one of awe, "it was a big aeroplane, with the cockpit some ten or so feet off the ground. A short set of steps let down from their concealed stowage in the side of the fuselage to enable one to start the climb to the cockpit and a further set of footholds, covered with spring-loaded doors, in the fuselage side facilitated the final ascent." Training began in the flight simulator, which was particularly important with regard to the starting procedure for the aircraft. A cartridge was fired to initiate a small turbine which then fired the main power unit. When starting from cold it was normally necessary to use a second cartridge to spool the engine up to the 4500 rpm required to enable it to continue to run under its own power. Timing was all, too early and the starter turbine would overspeed - with potentially disastrous and explosive consequences, too late and the whole business would have to be begun again. His first experience of flying the Gannet came on 2nd July in the T.2 XA520. Dual instruction was given by Lieutenant Reid in the centre cockpit, whose sole forward vision was by means of a periscope. After four sorties amounting to three hours and twenty minutes in total, he was sent off solo four days later, firstly in the same T.2 and then in the AS.1 WN429. Wilson later commented, "I just hoped nothing went wrong, for despite the dual instruction, the time spent in the simulator and assiduous study of the Pilot's Notes, I still only had the barest knowledge of what to do if it did." During the summer months of 1957 all flying involved a preliminary bus ride to RAF Ballykelly - as previously mentioned Eglinton's runways were being resurfaced. Training continued with formation flying, asymmetric handling (solo and in formation) and bombing with 25 lb practice charges on the range at Minearney beside Magilligan Point at the seaward end of Lough Foyle. The bomb sight was somewhat low-tech, being merely a chinagraph cross marked on the pilot's windscreen. Rocket projectile firing came next, by day and by night, when the "Glow Worm" target illuminators made an impressive show with the release of a magnesium flare which descended by parachute. On one occasion, during a night bombing exercise, a "Glow Worm" malfunctioned with the result that the brightly burning flare and its parachute became entangled with Gannet WN429's tailplane. Luckily the pilot was able to execute an emergency landing at Ballykelly in time for the crash crew to extinguish the blaze on what was left of the Gannet's smouldering tail. Another mishap was the time when a rocket launched itself while the aircraft was sitting on the apron. Fortunately it disappeared in the general direction of Lough Foyle without hitting anything on the way. In October 1957, the crew of WN358 had a fortunate escape when a Very pistol was set off inside the cockpit in flight over Magilligan Point.

After four months, Tony Wilson was deemed experienced enough to be allowed to fly with a crew of Observer, whose task was chiefly navigational and Telegraphist, who managed the operation of the sonobuoys. For this phase of the course he had moved to 719 NAS, still at Eglinton, of course. The work now consisted of learning how to use the aircraft's radar, sonar and weapons systems to search for, track and destroy submarines. Both passive and the much more expensive active sonobuoys were carried. A sonobuoy is a cylindrical device consisting of a flotation buoy, a hydrophone to detect noise in the water, and a radio transmitter to send the sonar signals back to the aircraft. When released, a small parachute retards its fall and on striking the water it releases the hydrophone, which sinks to the end of its cable. At the same time the aerial is erected and the buoy begins transmitting the sounds the hydrophone receives back to the aircraft. A pattern of sonobuoys is dropped, as in order to locate a submarine the operator needed to track more than one buoy. The relative strengths of return from each buoy could be used to calculate a fix on the target. A passive device listens to radiated noise from an underwater object while an active one transmits a sonar signal which reflects from the target rather like underwater radar.

Realistic exercises were carried out with submarines and frigates based at Londonderry, Royal Fleet Auxiliaries (RFAs) acting as mock convoys heading for Liverpool and the Ballykelly Shackletons. One night in November 1957, flying Gannet AS.1 WN438, has remained with Tony Wilson ever since, "it was filthy and black, with strong winds, torrential rain and low scudding cloud. My fellow trainees - observer and telegraphist - and I were briefed for a barrier patrol in the North Channel - eastward from Lough Foyle across to the Mull of Kintyre, then north-west to Islay and the Mull of Oa, eventually turning westward again back towards Malin Head on the coast of Donegal before setting off for the whole circuit again, at a height of 1000 feet, descending at times to 500 feet in an attempt to remain visual on the sea. On both sides of the Irish Sea our patrol line ended with a coastline rearing fairly steeply out of the sea and topped, close inland, by high hills. Only the recently learned radar interpretation and navigation skills of my trainee observer, Lieutenant Hawkins, kept us from impacting on something solid or wet. The tension was palpable as we drew closer to land at the end of each leg. At the end of the two hours and thirty-five minute sortie we gingerly felt our way back into the entrance to Lough Foyle. Through the darkness, cloud and rain, on the last leg, Ben Twitch to the left and the hills of Donegal to the right, I couldn't help but enquire a couple of times of Lieutenant Hawkins, was he absolutely certain that he had us lined up correctly on the radar? I just hoped that he was as confident as he sounded. At last the airfield lights came blearily into view and, as the wheels splashed down on the rain soaked runway, I reckoned that I'd earned my flying pay that day. So too had Lieutenant Hawkins!" At least Wilson had some forward vision through the rain streaked windscreen. Hawkins in the middle and the telegraphist in the back seat, Sub-Lieutenant Judd, were in dark little cocoons, illuminated only by the few dimmed red and ultra violet lights of their instruments and peering into stygian blackness on either side as they trusted to the skill of their nineteen years old Midshipman pilot.

A fortnight later, on 29th November, as he neared the end of the course, Tony Wilson flew Gannet AS.1 XA388 in company with his Observer, Sub-Lieutenant Husband and Leading Telegraphist Hind. Their mission was a daylight patrol exercise of the same area. He later described the events of the day, "The steady drone of our progress back and forth across the sea was broken by the acquisition of a faint radar contact a couple of miles ahead. As we drew closer a slightly larger splash of foam caught my eye and there, leaving a tell tale feather of spray in its wake, was the snorkel tube of a submarine running on its diesel engines, just below the surface. This was the moment that all our training so far had been leading up to. We didn't appear to have been spotted as we closed from astern, crossing his track at about 30 degrees. As Husband radioed off a sighting report, I opened the bomb door. In addition to our load of sonobuoys we carried Anti Submarine Training Indicators (ASTIs). These were similar to a hand grenade but filled with ball bearings, with insufficient explosive to damage the submarine. The rattling of the ball bearings on the hull plates when it exploded would indicate to the submariner that he had been attacked successfully. The chances of ever being in a similar position again were remote, so I selected a four bomb salvo from the eight carried and dived down in a text book depth charge attack. The ASTIs landed in a perfect straddle, one a little short and to starboard of the periscope wake, the next two either side of the snorkel and periscope, the fourth slightly ahead and to port of the line of advance. As we pulled out of the dive and climbed away the ASTIs exploded and the periscope and snorkel promptly disappeared. Only four small circles of foam indicated where our target had been a few moments before. We were all elated and claimed the sub as a "kill", though for the purposes of the exercise we went ahead and dropped patterns of sonobuoys for some 20 minutes, tracking our quarry until the arrival of another Gannet and a frigate." The outcome was less than satisfactory, as at the post-exercise debrief the submarine's commander flatly refused to accept that he had been "sunk". The three airmen came to the conclusion that he was a very bad sport. By the end of the year Tony Wilson had left Eglinton for a Gannet squadron at Culdrose but would return to the north-west of Ulster in due course.

In November 1957 Eglinton was reopened and the resident squadrons returned from Ballykelly. The runways and perimeter track had all been resurfaced but not extended. This work was completed ahead of schedule but the lighting installation had been delayed which left a large number of open trenches and "sundry other unnatural hazards" about the airfield, adding to the challenge of taxying - especially at night, when a vast number of glim lamps had to be laid to illuminate the perimeter track. The new approach lights to Runway 27 were installed by the beginning of 1958, at a cost of £500,000.

Also in November 719 had absorbed 737, and the name was changed to the Naval Anti-

Above: Gannets of 719 NAS
with engines running.
(D James)

Right: Fairey Gannet AS.1
XA352 of 719 NAS.
(D James)

Above: 815 NAS in 1956. David James was at that time the Senior Pilot
and is seated 4th from the left beside the CO Lieutenant Commander John
David. (D James)

Above: David James makes his farewell as CO to the members of 719 NAS. (D James)

Above: After making his speech, David was towed away in his old Standard 12 to his new place of duty, the control tower, to the accompaniment of many firecrackers. "Very emotional but great fun!". (D James)

Right: Bernadine was a great favourite of the CO's daughter. She liked sharing chocolate Wagon Wheels. (D James)

Submarine Operational Flying School. The squadron was augmented by the addition of three extra instructors and three Gannet T.2s. The requirement for Gannet trained aircrew was reducing as the Navy moved towards rotary-winged A/S aircraft. A brand new, purpose-built facility and hard standing suitable for accommodating the squadron personnel and aircraft, with all possible mod-cons, had been opened recently. Lieutenant Commander Jimmy James became the CO of 719, with its 12 Gannets, in December. His married quarters was a farmhouse near the airfield's perimeter and required only climbing over a small wall to get to work. The Squadron sent four aircraft to the Farnborough Air Show, where they were received very well. The IRA made its mark again by blowing up an unused concrete pill-box on the Magilligan Range, it was surmised that this rather futile choice of target was because it was a "passing-out" test for a "training class"!

Above: S Class Submarine and 815 NAS Whirlwind. (Tony Wilson)

Above: Captain Jameson addresses 820 NAS personnel on commissioning on 21st January 1958. (Author's Collection)

Right: One of the Federal German Navy Gannets which came to Eglinton in 1958. (Aeronauticum)

737 was not the only squadron to disband, as in the same month, 745 suffered the same fate. It had been reduced to two Avengers only in December 1956 and finished its life with two deployments on board HMS *Albion* and HMS *Bulwark*.

Lawrie McCarthy returned to Eglinton in January 1958, this time on the staff of 719. He was later commissioned and flew more than 1500 hours on Gannets.

On 21st January 1958 820 NAS, Lieutenant Commander FW Wilcox, reformed with eight Westland Whirlwind HAS.7s, three of which carried out a fly-past at the commissioning ceremony. It was the Royal Navy's first anti-submarine helicopter unit and remained at Eglinton until May when it embarked on board HMS *Eagle*. This was followed by 824 NAS, Lieutenant Commander J Trevis, on 21st April, also with A/S Whirlwinds. It joined HMS *Victorious* in August. No.1 German Anti-Submarine Squadron of the Federal German Navy was also formed just after Easter with 12 Gannet Mk.4s, under the command of Korvettenkapitan H Schopke, who had served in the Luftwaffe and had been taken as a prisoner of war. They had commenced training on the Gannet at Fairey's airfield, White Waltham, in February. Many years later one of the squadron members, now retired Flottillenadmiral Paul Kriebel, recalled that they came "as former enemies and left as friends, due to the fact that both parties, British and German, were determined that, just over a decade after the war, prejudices had to be overcome in good naval manner." He paid tribute to the part that Lieutenant Commander James played in making them feel at home. The *Derry Standard* reported at some length on the commissioning ceremony which took place on 20th May. Vice Admiral Ruge, the Inspector-General of the Federal German Navy conclued his speeech by saying, "This ceremony today is a step in the right direction which we hope will lead to lasting peace for the nations and freedom in our Western way of life. I can assure you that this is deeply felt in Germany." It was a matter of some pleasure for the A/S School that the Squadron decided to incorporate a Gannet of the feathered kind in its official crest. It is also of interest to note that of the 26 German naval officers who participated in this course between April and July 1958, two became admirals and eight attained the rank of captain. As 814, Lieutenant Commander R Fulton, and subsequently, Lieutenant Commander JJ Philips, was also at Eglinton during that period, for some weeks the Station was host to five squadrons - four first line and one second line. 719 was chiefly engaged in the training Commonwealth Officers. The Squadron offices also suffered from a rodent problem, as proven by a photograph of a very small mouse balanced on the lip of the CO's tea-cup. The Station diary noted that, "for a time Eglinton resumed something of its old-remembered character." On 20th May, Commander (Air) CK Roberts DSO was promoted to Captain and took over from Captain TGC Jameson.

A mouse caught sabotaging the CO of 719's cuppa. (Author's Collection)

Locally based frigates were becoming a scarce commodity for A/S training. The situation was

Above: Gannets and personnel of 824 NAS. (JD Honeywill)

Left: Grumman TBM-3 Avengers of the Royal Netherlands Navy. (RNN)

Above: A formation of 719 NAS Gannets. (D James)

Right: Gannets of the Federal German Navy. (Aeronauticum)

improved somewhat by the transfer of the First Seaward Defence Boat Squadron from Portland to Derry during the winter of 1957-58. The first to arrive was HMS *Camberford*. The weather during that winter was very severe resulting in a very snowy backdrop to 820's commissioning ceremony. It also brought more work for the helicopters. A Station Flight Dragonfly was called to assist the crew of a Dutch freighter, the *Saba*, which had run aground on the Donegal coast. A Whirlwind from 820 was sent to remove a lighthouse-keeper suffering from appendicitis off Inistrahull. This was a particularly tricky rescue as it was carried out by night.

Lt Cdr Eric Meadowcroft flew two rescue missions to the Dutch freighter *Saba* on 9th December 1957 in the Dragonfly 916 firstly with CPO Ruddock and then with PO Childs (Lt Cdr E Meadowcroft via Raymond Burrows Collection).

After the departure of the German Gannets to their base at Jagel in Schleswig, a further overseas visitor, in July, was No.2 Royal Netherlands Naval Squadron, Lieutenant Commander Seret, with six Avengers for a period of weapons training. They were followed by No.4 Squadron, Lieutenant Van Worden. Both were accompanied by two Dakotas

The Whirlwind XK935 of 820 NAS had to make a forced landing near the Giant's Causeway on 12th March 1958. (High McGrattan)

carrying spare parts and other stores. It was noted that, "Anglo-Dutch relations were reaffirmed in both professional and social spheres."

Later in the summer the final Air Day was blessed with good weather and was a resounding success, attracting a record attendance - evidence of the esteem in which the Station was held. The finale was a set piece assault by the Royal Marines supported by Sea Hawks from Lossiemouth screaming overhead, "together with a huge number of the large bangs and flashes beloved by the Irish public." It was one of several events billed as "The Last" - the Summer Ball, the Station Christmas Dance to name but two. The 1958 Defence Estimates had disclosed that several naval air stations would close by 1961, including Ford, Bramcote, Brawdy and Worthy Down as well as Eglinton.

Several incidents took place in 1958. A Whirlwind from 820 NAS, XK935, suffered engine trouble and had to make a forced landing in a field near the Giant's Causeway. On 25th May another Westland Whirlwind HAS Mk.7 XK934 of 820 NAS ditched off Inishowen Head. The three crew members, Lieutenant Springall, Lieutenant Glass and Leading Seaman Duncan, were picked up by the frigate HMS *Zest*. Subsequent efforts made to locate and salvage the aircraft were unsuccessful. Not to be outdone, a Gannet of 814 NAS, XA426, was taxying when wheels-up was selected, causing quite an amount of damage.

On 1st October 815 NAS reformed, commanded by Lieutenant Commander HM Hayes, with twelve Whirlwind HAS 7s to operate as the Naval Air Anti-Submarine School (Rotary Wing). The training programme consisted of three weeks at HMS *Vernon* and HMS *Osprey* followed by 14 weeks crew training with 815, after which complete crews of pilot, observer and crewman would be ready for appointment in A/S squadrons. No.1 Course, consisting of seven full crews, joined in mid-October. The advent of the A/S helicopter was noted as being of tremendous importance to the Royal Navy, "even in its present crude form it has great tactical potential; with its full all-weather capability it will become one of the most complex pieces of aviation machinery, some say, also the most expensive; others, the most frightening."

It got off to an unfortunate start. On 21st October a Whirlwind, XL877, from 815 crashed into the sea after the pilot lost control due to a failure of the transmission or flying controls. Lieutenant JM Shrives later stated, "We were hovering at about 20 feet above the sea when the aircraft began to give trouble. I realised we would have to ditch it. While I tried to control it as best I could, "Mayday" distress signals were sent out and picked up by two other helicopters in the area. The signals were relayed to Eglinton, which immediately sent out two SAR helicopters." The helicopter was taking part with other aircraft and ships in an A/S exercise ten miles out in the Atlantic off Inishowen Head. Its distress signals were also heard by the Dutch submarine *Zeeleeuw*, which surfaced to pick up the airmen, Lieutenants Shrives, IAC Cobbold and TR Coombs, from their dinghies after only ten minutes in the water. Two Dragonfly SAR helicopters were sent from Eglinton to rendezvous with the submarine and winch up the rescued crew.

This was followed a week later by another Whirlwind, XL869, from the same squadron ditching after engine failure. The Whirlwind, another Westland licence-built development of a Sikorsky design, this time the S-55, was in effect the replacement for the Dragonfly. The

Lt Eric Taylor with the 'clipped wing' Gannet AS.1 WN349 550GN of 719 NAS. (Agusta Westland)

Mk.7 was powered by an Alvis Leonides piston engine and had a reputation of being rather prone to mechanical failure. This was possibly due to the fact that it was installed to rotate in the opposite direction to the original design which had an adverse effect on the lubrication system. On a lighter note, the Operations Officer was on the receiving end of a telephone call from a local Coastguard Station which reported as follows,

"One of your helicopters anchored off the coast about two minutes ago, I thought you would like to know .... but it's all right, he's just pulling up his anchor and flying away now. " It would appear that the lowering and raising of the dunking sonar had caused this confusion.

On 25th November 1958 Lieutenant ES Taylor was flying Gannet WN349 engaged in a high-speed, 38-degree rocket firing dive on the range at Minearney when he had a very lucky escape. It is believed that he inadvertently flew through the slipstream of the previous attacking aircraft just as he was pulling out of his dive. The strain on the wings of the Gannet was so great that the outer sections of both wings broke off simultaneously. Despite the fact that the ailerons had thereby been lost, the pilot maintained control and made a safe landing back at Eglinton with his very relieved crewman, LRO (Air) PJ Watson - a tribute not only to Taylor's flying skills but also to the robust nature and inherent stability of the Gannet. The following day one of the station SAR Helicopter Flight's Dragonflys, WN498, set off with the aim of recovering the missing wing sections from the mud at low water. It was flown by the

Dragonfly WN498 which ditched in November 1958. (Inset: Lt Cdr Eric Meadowcroft) (both Lt Cdr E Meadowcroft via Raymond Burrows Collection)

Commanding Officer of 815 SAR Flight, Lieutenant Commander "Porky" Meadowcroft, a charming, kindly and well-rounded man. As the helicopter hovered low over the scene the crewman lowered the hook of the rescue winch down to the party below, which had affixed canvas strops to one of the wing sections. With the wing dangling below, the pilot raised the collective to apply power. Unfortunately the hollow spaces inside the wing were filled with sand, mud and sea water with the result that more and more power was applied to little avail. Moreover the cyclic was being held over hard to starboard to counteract the weight dragging from the portside winch. It seemed to the crewman that the aircraft would shortly nose down into the sea on top of the wing and accompanying personnel. He therefore exercised his initiative and cut the cable by prompt use of the emergency system. Sadly he was so prompt that this took the pilot completely by surprise, with the result that the helicopter reared nose up, rolled rapidly to starboard (with full pressure still on the cyclic) and crashed into the sludge a few feet below. Thankfully there were no serious injuries but it would have been interesting to hear Lieutenant Commander Meadowcroft's next words to his crewman on the subject of timely and appropriate communications. The SAR Flight had lost 50% of its aircraft strength but worse was to follow a week or two later. Lieutenant "Chunky" Allen was flying the remaining helicopter when he spied a friendly fishing boat just off the coast. He hovered above and lowered a consignment of Aircrew Emergency Rations (sealed tins of sweets and chewing gum issued on a regular basis) and in return hoisted a wastepaper basket filled with freshly caught fish. The day only got worse from there on as, very soon afterwards, the helicopter suffered a clutch failure and had to be ditched, wiping out the entire remaining Flight. Luckily plenty of spare Dragonflys were to be had from storage, three of which, WG667, WN499 and WG722 were delivered by the time a new pilot, Sub-Lieutenant Tony Wilson, arrived in January 1959. He had converted from Gannets and was soon at work on the day to day business of the Flight - chiefly in the communications role, carrying senior officers from place to place, taking range marking officers out to Minearney or Magilligan Point. Now and again there were practice winch exercises, photographic sorties, air experience flights for ground crew or other members of Eglinton's ship's company and also the transfer of personnel to and from naval vessels off the coast. Tony Wilson transferred from the SAR Flight to 815 Squadron. The accident-prone Whirlwind HAS 7s were withdrawn in March 1959 and were replaced by HAR 3s which were fitted with R-1300-3 Wright Cyclone engines. It was decided to move the squadron to Portland Naval Base in Dorset, where a new heliport had been constructed and on 14th April 1959 they too departed from Eglinton. One of the eight departing helicopters was flown by Tony's squadron colleague, George White. He remembers it as one long day of four legs, with an extra stop at Sydenham to refuel before the sea crossing to Ronaldsway because as he explained, "All my Mark 3 flying to that date had been in the local circuit or hovering for which the standard operating procedure was to maintain rich mixture. Everyone else somehow had got the message to lean off the mixture for cruising. By Belfast I had 100 lbs less fuel than the rest."

At the end of the year, the final batch of trainees for the fixed-wing A/S School arrived, a contingent of observers from the Indian Navy. In its final few months, naturally, there were no more British students, apart from those on the Gannet Conversion Course and the final Air Weapons Instructor Course. The Gannets still flew intensively, receiving frequent requests to participate in A/S exercises, firing range surveillance and long-range SAR missions.

Jimmy James became Lieutenant Commander (Air) in January 1959. Doubtless he too was faced with a growing phenomenon, "emerging here in increasing numbers, known as the Two-or Three-Hatted Officer. The expression "drafted without relief" confronts us more and more frequently and the filling of vacated chairs with remaining staff is an ever-present problem." Despite the shortcomings of the Whirlwind Mk.7 the first seven crews trained by the A/S School (Rotary Wing) joined their squadrons as planned in January. The second course which, in the best traditions of the Service, was entitled No.3 Course began training with the reduced complement of Whirlwind Mk.3s. Ten of the German Gannets along with 18 officers and 80 ratings returned to Eglinton in February and stayed until the middle of March, undertaking weapons training. The CO was Korvettenkapitan Paul Kriebel. By 17th March the final fixed-wing course had come to an end and time was nearly up for Eglinton's Gannets. On 29th April of that year James was responsible for the following signal to Flag Officer Flying Training (FOFT):

Gannet's Lament *or* **Foyled at Last**

Our flying task is finished after 15 years or more,
And the Air Arm's days are ended on this Emerald Island's shore,
From Swordfish through to Gannets with choppers last in line,
The crews have downed their Guinness at Issue Centre 9.
We've been laying up our ensign in the parish church today,
And we've briefed the last two aircraft and set them on their way,
The day is April 29, 1600 now,
We're off the air and closing down this is our final bow."
The following morning FOFT replied in kind:
"Twas sad indeed to whittle away
A fine air station yesterday
Now Navy's aircraft wheels will rush
No more through Irish grasses lush
But Air Arm men may soon forget
The joys of Guinness strong and wet
Though memories will linger on
Of great times spent at Eglinton
And may nostalgia mix with pride
On oceans and through air space wide."

It was an important base - the centre of excellence or alma mater for anti-submarine warfare, along with JASS and Ballykelly nearby. Geographically it was in the right location during the Cold War.

A farewell service was held at Eglinton Parish Church, where a packed congregation listened to the Rector, Reverend CD Morgan, pay tribute to the men and women of the Air Station - "The part the personnel of the Station have played in the social life of the community has been tremendous. They enjoyed themselves in making enjoyment for others. In village affairs their help was freely available and when it was asked for no more willing and efficient assistance could be desired. They will be greatly missed, not only in Eglinton but in the North-West generally. Many of them have worshipped in this church, some of the children have been baptised here, many young couples have been married within these walls and in the hallowed ground surrounding the church there are the graves of some of those who in war and peace gave their lives in the service of Queen and country." The White Ensign for laying up in the church was handed over by the Commanding Officer, Captain CK Roberts. Before the service the Flag Officer Air (Home) Admiral Sir Walter Couchman, himself a former CO at Eglinton, inspected a guard of honour drawn up on the road facing the church. RN and RM personnel lined the pathway from the road to the main entrance. Another former CO, Captain TWB Shaw was also present, in his capacity as Deputy Air

Officer Flying Training.

Eglinton was left in the hands of the de-storing party, who had a mammoth job packing and removing all the portable items accumulated over nearly twenty years.

Many were sad to see the station close, despite never ending remarks about the Irish weather and the soft Ulster rain. Thousands of naval personnel had served there and many had come to love its unique qualities. It is said if you hadn't been there you regarded a posting as being to the end of the world but if you loved sport of all kinds, wild fowling, fishing and beautiful scenery it was the place for you. In general those with a country background thrived while those who were townies at heart hated it. The quarters may have been untouched since the war and needing a lick of paint but the atmosphere was very friendly. People made their own fun and the wardroom was active and lively. The pubs and restaurants of Coleraine, Portrush, Londonderry (the County Hotel and the Atlantic Bar were favourites), as well as those at Buncrana, Muff, Moville and Letterkenny over the border in Co.Donegal, were at hand.

The view of many of those serving at Eglinton was well-summarised as follows,

> "The closure has come just when a start has been made to bring the facilities up to a modern standard. A number of new buildings have been constructed on the airfield recently and only a bare two years ago the airfield was closed for six months for renovation of the runways, perimeter tracks and airfield lighting. To the local civilian population it was a great shock and a matter of particular regret that the links of the Fleet Air Arm and Northern Ireland are to be almost completely severed after their close association over many years."

It was regarded throughout the Navy as being more unconventional then any other Air Station. Some stories are shrouded in the mists of time,

> "The Wren "O" who, clad only in a raincoat, went over the border to collect her new tweed suit. Is it true that an alert Customs Officer suspected something as he followed her to the upper deck of a bus? The "person unknown" who left a very senior officer tied up with his pyjama cord outside "The Cottage". The Air Day when the crowd cheered madly as No.4 chewed up his leader's rudder, spraying the pieces into Nos. 2 and 3. The Carrier Air Group syndicate which won the football pools. Whatever one thought on that long trek from Ark Royal to Anson site on a rainy day, there was always something about Eglinton. One feels that in the future

Left: Whirlwind HAS Mk 7 XN 357 of 719 NAS. It joined the squadron in May 1960 and crashed on 7th February 1961. (David Hill)

Above: Wessex HAS 1 XP 145 of 819 NAS over the Giant's Causeway in June 1963. This crashed on 4th October 1963. (David Hill)

Eglinton will be spoken of with the same nostalgia and near-reverence accorded by really aged Naval Aviators to Hatston (HMS *Sparrowhawk*), Twatt (HMS *Tern*) and Machrihanish (HMS *Landrail*)."

The great days at Eglinton were over. Part of the airfield was reactivated in 1960 as HMS *Sea Eagle* for helicopters in support of JASS. 719 NAS was reformed on 17th May and equipped with three Whirlwind HAS Mk.7s for this purpose. Flying commenced on 24th May and all three helicopters were available by the end of the month. A Whirlwind was lost on 7th February 1961 when it had to ditch. On 5th October the Squadron was accorded first line status and become 819 NAS, re-equipping with four Wessex HAS.1s. The commissioning ceremony was attended by Vice-Admiral DP Dreyer, Flag Officer Air (Home) and the Senior Naval officer Northern Ireland, Captain EN Sinclair.

The helicopters' task was perhaps not just limited to the A/S training role. It may be also that they kept a sharp lookout for "fishing trawlers" festooned with antennae which loitered about observing JASS activities and also the approaches to the Faslane submarine base. Aid to the civil community

Above and left: Coleraine February 1963: Wessex XM916 of 819 NAS assists with milk deliveries during the 'Big Snow'. This aircraft served from Oct 1961 to Sep 1965 which was a relatively long period of time as no less than seven Wessex Mk 1s were lost during the six-and-a-half years the type was with 819 NAS. (Hugh McGrattan)

was also given, particularly with drops of fodder to livestock during the harsh winter of 1963. On 22nd January six Electricity Board engineers were flown to a remote hilltop in the Sperrins to carry out repairs on an important transmitter, the whole area around which being covered with deep snowdrifts – one of the last operations from Eglinton. Two days later a maildrop was made to RFA *Tideflow* near the mouth of Lough Foyle, when the bag was winched up again half a bottle of rum was found inside as "payment" for services rendered. It then moved to a purpose built facility at RAF Ballykelly in February 1963, the naval presence at Eglinton coming to an end. The Squadron's Operational Record Book (ORB) has the following entry for 1st February, "The squadron started to move items from Eglinton to Ballykelly. Two lorries were employed in moving bulk items. This is the last full working day of the squadron at RNAS Eglinton and therefore the last Navy link with the station is being broken."

Above: Emerald Airways' first service from Eglinton to Glasgow in September 1966. (Hugh McGratton)

That was not the end of the Eglinton story as the airfield was reopened for civil use when the new local airline Emerald Airways took out a five year lease. The runways were re-surfaced and a small passenger terminal was constructed. Sadly services by Emerald Airways were short-lived. Following a proving flight with

Above: 32 (R) Sqn BAe146 at the airport. (City of Derry Airport)

Above: Aerial view of the airport (City of Derry Airport)

Left: Approaching City of Derry Airport in a Trislander of Woodgate Air Charter. (Guy Warner)

Below left: A BAE 146 of Manx Airlines on the ramp at City of Derry Airport. (City of Derry Airport)

Below: A SAAB 340 of BA franchise holder Loganair at City of Derry Airport. (Alex Brand)

The first arrival at the new terminal in 1994 was a Loganair Shorts 360. (City of Derry Airport)

the DH Heron G-AOZN from Shannon (SNN) via Aldergrove (BFS) on 29th June, a weekly service to Prestwick was commenced on 1st July. The first flight of a daily schedule from Aldergrove to Glasgow, Abbotsinch via Eglinton was flown using Heron G-ALZL on 16th September 1966. Short Skyvans and DC-3s were also used in the winter of 1966-67 but by November 1967 the company had gone out of business.

Eglinton Flying Club took over responsibility for running the airfield at Eglinton from the late sixties by leasing land from the various landowners who continued to own the runways following the Navy's withdrawal.

In 1978 Derry City Council took over the operation of the Airport with the intention of improving the transport infrastructure for the north-west (including the Irish Republic). This was a bold and forward thinking decision which took time to really get off the ground. Scottish airline, Loganair, started a service to Glasgow (GLA) in 1979. Then in May 1981, the Irish airline, Avair, began flying to Dublin (DUB). Over the next number of years other operators came and went on the Dublin schedule - Air Arann, Shannon Executive Aviation, Iona National Airways, Aer Lingus, Jersey European Airways, Air Arann (again) and Loganair as a British Airways franchise route. Loganair has flown a wide range of aircraft (on a number of routes Glasgow, Manchester, Dublin, Blackpool (BLK) and the Isle of Man (IOM)) including Britten-Norman Islanders and Trislanders, DHC-6 Twin Otters, Short 330s and 360s, BAe Jetstream 41s and now Saab 340s.

Seamus Devine arrived at the airport in 1987 as an Air Traffic Control officer and since 1988 has been the airport manager, overseeing a time of great change. In 1989 a service to Manchester (MAN) was commenced, operated by BA franchise holders with types including

BAe ATPS, 146s, Jetstream 41s and Saab 340s. On 9th January 1994 a smart new terminal building with a modern fire station alongside was opened and the airport was renamed City of Derry (LDY). Moreover in order to cope easily with aircraft up to the size of a Boeing 757 or Airbus A321, the main runway 08/26 (which has a length of 1852 metres) has been considerably re-built, strengthened, re-profiled, modernised and upgraded. A total of £10.5 million was spent improving the airport's facilities, with 75% grant aid coming from the European Union and 25% from Derry City Council. Passenger numbers were still only about 40,000 a year. A new airline, Macair, arrived in 1995 with services to Stansted (STN), Birmingham (BHX) and Edinburgh (EDI), but sadly it did not last long. Also in 1995 Jersey European Airways introduced a five times daily service to Belfast which linked into their network to and from Belfast City Airport (BHD). By 1997 the annual number of passengers had risen but only to 56,000. The JEA service terminated in 1998.

In 1997 the Swiss airline, Crossair, began a summer charter series to Zurich with the Saab 2000. On 1st July 1999 came a highly significant move, Ryanair began a service to STN with Boeing 737-200s (the first being EI-CKQ) and more recently with the larger 737-800s. From 2001 the LDY – DUB route has benefitted from a Public Service Obligation (PSO) subsidy from the Irish Government, which has been renewed until 2008. Passenger numbers in the 21st century have risen steadily from the 200,000 achieved for the first time in 2002. Air Arann returned to City of Derry in 2004-05 with schedules to MAN and BHX. Ryanair added Liverpool (LPL) in February 2006, Nottingham East Midlands (EMA) in April and Prestwick (PIK) in December of the same year. The City of Derry Airport is thriving with scheduled services to STN, LPL, EMA, GLA, PIK and DUB. Holiday charter services will be flown to a variety of European destinations including Majorca, Lanzarote, Barcelona and Faro by Eirjet, Air 2000 and LTE International, using Airbus A320s and Boeing 737s. Passenger numbers for 2006 are estimated at 400,000.

Ryanair Boeing 737-200 EI-COB at City of Derry on a proving flight on 4th May 1999. (Jack Woods)

Jersey European Airways Short 360 G-OBHD lands at City of Derry in 1996.
(Guy Warner)

As an historical footnote it is of interest to note that the first commercial flights between Belfast and Londonderry were operated briefly in the summer of 1925 between Malone and Gransha by Northern Airlines and were given financial support by the Chamber of Commerce. This was the first internal air service in Ireland. A timetable of 18th May 1925 gives the following schedule:

Depart: Stranraer 6.30 am - arrive: Belfast 7.00 am - d. Belfast 7.15 am - a. Derry 8.15 am - d. Derry 5.00 pm - a. Belfast 6.15 pm - d. Belfast 7.30 pm - a. Stranraer 8.00 pm.

One untoward incident took place, when the DH9 G-EBJX was compelled to make a forced landing at Limavady, when returning to Belfast from Londonderry. The aircraft was dismantled where it landed, brought by road to Belfast, repaired and reassembled. Not long after this, the last service was flown on 8th June 1925.

The Northern Airlines DH9 G-EBJX which made a forced landing at Limavady in 1925 (Belfast Telegraph)

CHAPTER 4

— ∘O∘ —

Some more naval matters

Ballykelly

No sooner had the Wessex of 819 NAS arrived at Ballykelly in February 1963 than they departed again for RNAS Brawdy by way of a re-fuelling stop at RAF Valley en-route for exercises on board the aircraft carrier HMS *Centaur*. While at Brawdy the helicopters carried out several snow relief sorties before flying to *Centaur* on 7th February. Barely two hours later, in answer to an urgent request from the Northern Ireland Government, they took off again for Ballykelly.

The *Belfast Telegraph* reported on 11th February, "Naval aircrews at Ballykelly have saved hundreds of starving sheep by dropping tons of hay in the past three days. The crews have been in the air for 58 hours on their flights of mercy. One of the aircraft operated from Aldergrove and the other two from Ballykelly. Fodder was also dropped near Ballycastle after fog and low cloud had made it impossible for a Hastings from 202 Squadron at Aldergrove to undertake the mission." The bales of hay weighed 40 lbs each and a load of some 1500 lbs was carried per trip, with the sonar gear and back seats removed. The ORB noted, "Considerable work with vacuum cleaners was needed to remove the hay from the insides of the aircraft."

On Wednesday 13th February the Flag Officer Flying Training, Rear Admiral PD Gick, arrived in his Hunting Sea Prince "barge" to open the new squadron buildings, work on which was still in progress. A few days later squadron aircraft exercised for the first time with a nuclear submarine out of Holy Loch, the USS *Ethan Allen*.

The Shackletons continued to fly from RAF Ballykelly. Regular visitors in the 1960s included the Gannet ECM.6s and Sea Venom 21/22 ECMs of 831 NAS for electronic countermeasures training and exercise, while the Ballykelly Station Flight consisted of a Vickers Varsity, WF331 and Hunting Pembroke, WV739. Other naval visitors included DH Sea Vixens and Fairey Gannets on exercise. Sadly in 1962, two Gannets from 831 NAS flying in formation in cloud, flew straight into one of the hills adjacent to Ballykelly, killing all the six crew on the two aircraft. Tony Wilson described the experience of operating from Ballykelly in adverse conditions thus, "On those frequent days when the weather turned grim, with low cloud, mists and rain settling in, a great deal of concentration went into flying in and

Above: Shackleton MR2 Phase 3 WR967 and Wessex HAS Mk 3 XP118 at Ballykelly in 1970. (David Hill)

Left: The RAF Medical Officer of Health arrives at Portrush in 1969 in Wasp HAS1 XS532 from HMS Hecate. (Hugh McGrattan)

out of there and many were the sweaty palms experienced on some of those black, claggy nights that wrapped themselves around us." The Federal German Navy also sent three or four of its Gannets to Ballykelly every year to participate in anti-submarine warfare courses at Londonderry. The squadron had moved from Schleswig/Jagel to Westerland/Isle of Sylt in 1962 and then to Nordholz/Cuxhaven in 1964. Its normal duties included reconnaissance over the Baltic and North Seas, as well as taking part in NATO exercises until the Gannet was retired from active service in 1966.

Above: Wessex HAS Mk 3 XP143 of 819 NAS Ballykelly in 1969. (R Mackenzie)

The Wessex HAS 1s of 819 NAS were replaced by HAS 3s in April 1968. Then at the close of the year 1969 JASS was transferred from Londonderry to Turnhouse in Scotland. The Wessex had quite a limited endurance, so when the Squadron was operating in the North Channel a fuel bowser would be sent along the coast to Ballycastle for re-fuelling and changing crews in a handy field. At other times operations were conducted out of Prestwick if

Gazelle AH.1 XX 392 B of 3CBAS in the grounds of Altnagelvin Hospital on 14th April 1980. (David Hill)

the submarines with which the Wessex were exercising were in the Firth of Clyde. In July 1970 the Squadron embarked in RFA *Tidepool* and took part in exercises with submarines all the way to Gibraltar. Most of the aircrew flew back to Belfast with BEA, leaving the three embarked aircraft to come back by sea. In January 1971 819 NAS also departed for Culdrose. Finally on 31st March the Shackletons of No.204 Squadron RAF left Ballykelly, which was handed over to the Army in June and renamed Shackleton Barracks. Henceforth the principal aviation assets based at Ballykelly were those of the Army Air Corps - Sioux, Gazelle, Scout and Lynx - the last of which departed in 1991. During those years Ballykelly also played host to the Sioux of 40 and 42 Commando in 1971-72 and the Gazelles of 3 Commando Brigade Air Squadron in the period 1978-80.

HARLAND AND WOLFF

The story of naval aviation in Ulster would not be complete without mention of the aircraft carriers and other aviation capable ships which were constructed at Harland and Wolff 's shipyard in Belfast. They were, in alphabetical order, HMCS *Bonaventure* (which was bought by the Royal Canadian Navy - its McDonnell F2H-3 Banshees made a noisy visit to Sydenham in the autumn of 1957), HMS *Bulwark*, HMS *Campania* (a wartime escort carrier converted from the uncompleted hull of a refrigerated cargo ship), HMS *Centaur*, HMS *Eagle*, HMS *Formidable*, HMS *Glorious*, HMS *Glory*, HMCS *Magnificent*, HMS *Unicorn*, and HMS *Warrior*. To this list may be added: HMS *New Zealand*, a 45,000 ton Gibraltar class carrier, which was cancelled at the end of the war; the pre-war, catapult-equipped cruisers; HMS *Belfast*, HMS *Penelope* and then post-war; the assault ship HMS *Fearless*; the destroyer HMS *Kent*, frigates HMS *Berwick*, HMS *Leander*, HMS *Charybdis* and Royal Fleet Auxiliary vessels RFA *Regent* and RFA *Fort Victoria* – which were all capable of operating helicopters. Moreover, two particulary significant vessels were converted by the yard for naval duties; firstly in 1967-68 the MV *Anita Dan* was transformed into the ice patrol ship HMS *Endurance* and then in 1984-87 the MV *Contender Bezant* was re-built as the aviation training ship RFA *Argus*.

SHORTS

It would be wrong not to include in this account the two naval aircraft designed and built by Short Brothers in Belfast.

Some Belfast-built naval vessels.

Above: RFA Regent
Right: Launch of HMS Belfast
Right middle: HMS Eagle
(all Belfast Telegraph)

Above middle: HMS Bulwark
Above lower: HMS Kent
(both Belfast Telegraph)
Right bottom: HMCS Bonaventure 1957
(www.underthecat.com)

THE STURGEON

The Sturgeon was originally intended as a reconnaissance bomber for operations against Japan but with the construction of new aircraft carriers suspended at the end of the war, the requirement no longer existed. It was the first twin-engine aircraft designed expressly to a Royal Naval specification for carrier operations. In this role it would have been armed with bombs or depth charges. It was subsequently developed as a high-speed target-tug for air-to-air firing by day or night, photographic marking, throw-off target practice and marking and radar calibration. An extended nose held one camera position with the other being located dorsally aft of the wings. A towing winch and target stowage were also incorporated. The second prototype was the Sturgeon 1 RK791 which was a gunnery trainer and flew from Sydenham in 1948 under the designation SA2. It formed the basis for the main production model the TT Mk2 of which 23 entered service with the Royal Navy. It was powered by a pair of 1440 hp Merlin engines driving contra-rotating propellers. The *Aeroplane* magazine described it as, "a gentleman's aircraft, viceless in practically every way.....with a delightfully roomy and cosily sunk cockpit in a well between the wings." It began sea trials aboard HMS *Illustrious* in June 1950. In July and August 1951 three Sturgeons, TS477, TS483 and TS484 of 703 NAS flew from Eglinton and Sydenham, taking part in developing the prototype steam catapult trials which were being carried out onboard HMS *Perseus*. The aircraft were launched several times from the carrier moored at Airport Wharf, Sydenham before the sea trials.

They subsequently performed usefully, towing winged or sleeved targets for ship-to-air and air-to-air firing, flying from Malta amongst other bases. On sorties two aircraft were routinely used, one acting as a camera ship to record the results.

Shorts TT Mk 2 Sturgeon landing on HMS Illustrious in July 1950. (Aeroplane www. aeroplanemonthly. com)

The final Sturgeon was the S.B.3, WF632, a competitor for the Gannet in the anti-submarine, radar search and patrol roles. It was powered by two Armstrong Siddeley Mamba turboprops and flew on 12th August 1950. It was a deeply ugly looking machine with a bulbous nose, which provided the accommodation for a search radar and two operators.

THE SEAMEW

The SB6 Seamew was a rather quaint looking aeroplane. It was intended as a lightweight, turboprop anti-submarine aircraft. The prototype, XA209, first flew on 23rd August 1953 and made its debut at Farnborough the same year. The test pilot on both occasions was Squadron Leader WJ "Wally" Runciman AFC, DFM. The philosophy behind its design was described in the *Shorts Quarterly Review*, "The continued tendency for military aircraft of all types to grow larger and more complicated is creating an immense economic problem of increasing importance to those countries forming the North Atlantic Treaty Organisation. Somehow this trend has got to be checked. Within the last ten years aircraft have trebled their weight and costs have soared. For each unit of additional weight a larger wing is needed to lift it, a larger fuel tank is needed to feed the engine and to hold all this a more solid structure is essential."

The aim was to provide the navy with larger numbers of cheaper aircraft. Indeed the RN described the project as, "an attempt to bring the good old cheap Swordfish concept up to date, particularly for use by RNVR Squadrons and able to operate off the smallest aircraft carriers." One of the prime movers behind this idea was Rear Admiral Matthew Slattery, the Chairman and Managing Director of Shorts, who had also been the Director of Naval Supply (Air). He was first appointed to the Board of the company in 1948, becoming in due course Managing Director and then Chairman in 1952. His

Seamew landing (top), being stowed (middle) and ready for take-off from HMS Bulwark July 1955 (Bombardier Belfast)

Seamew and Swordfish at a Sydenham Airshow in the mid 1950s.
(Bombardier Belfast)

influence on the company was immense during his twelve years of dedicated service. He encouraged the diversification which ensured the survival of the company during a difficult decade.

Going back to the Seamew, carrier deck landing trials were carried out on board HMS *Bulwark* (also constructed in Belfast) in July 1955. A few months later, in October, two Seamews, XE169 and XA213, were sent to sea on board HMS *Warrior* for an intensive programme of deck-landing trials. Some 200 deck-landings and 50 catapult launches were split between the two aircraft. The programme was completed successfully, it was reported that, "For those of you who will fly the Seamew, it is one of the easiest deck-landing aircraft ever and the undercarriage is the softest yet." There was only one untoward incident when a defective hood lock came undone on one of the catapult launches, "the ship's AEO, who was gallantly sitting in the rear seat working the recorders, found himself airborne in the open with streamers of paper from the recorder waving around him. However, it caused him no more damage than fright."

The Seamew was designed to a government specification for operation from small carriers, dictating slow approach speeds, with crisp handling but at the same time having the structural strength for relatively high diving speeds for submarine attack. The typical full-flap stall speed was 48 knots (88 kph) with a maximum diving speed in excess of 270 knots (497 kph). The Seamew had a crew of two and was powered by an Armstrong Siddeley Mamba turboprop. A contemporary report stated,

> "In the air it gives the impression of being nose heavy, the result of placing both pilot and radar as close to the nose as possible for most efficient working. Engine, pilot and radar scanner are virtually stacked one upon the other, the pilot being seated over the engine with the radar scanner suspended below it. The structure of the fuselage was evolved particularly to withstand the loads imposed by ditching without nosing over or breaking up; the watertight floor of the crew compartment extends the whole length of the fuselage to provide adequate flotation and actually forms the roof of the capacious weapons bay. As a weight saving measure, it has a fixed undercarriage."

Only a small number had been accepted by the Royal Navy when the project was cancelled. Tragically, on 9th June 1956, Wally Runciman was killed when Seamew XE175 crashed at the Sydenham Air Display. As a concept, the Seamew was an interesting idea that ultimately did not really work. Though in fairness, it should be added that the notorious Defence Cuts of 1957 did not help. The intention had been that the simplicity of the Seamew lent itself to operation by Fleet Air Arm and RAF Coastal Command auxiliaries - these, of course, fell victim to the Treasury's axe. No example of the Seamew was preserved, though the Ulster Aviation Society does have a cockpit canopy.

SYDENHAM

In 1946 Sydenham had become a civilian-manned RN Aircraft Maintenance Yard. The Superintendant of the Yard also held a dormant appointment as the Commanding Officer RNAS Belfast, which became HMS *Gannet* III and a satellite of Eglinton. This appointment lapsed in 1958. In 1947 the repair and reconditioning of naval aircraft began in earnest, on Sea Otters and Barracudas. An engine repair shop was also set up for the overhaul of Rolls-Royce engines. It was renamed Royal Naval Aircraft Yard (RNAY) Sydenham in 1953, a sister establishment to Donibristle and Fleetlands. The main work at this time was on Fireflies, which continued until 1956. The first jet type was the Sea Hawk in 1955. The new generation of naval aircraft was also to include Sea Venoms, Sturgeons, Hunters, Sea Vixens, Sea Herons, Sea

From top: Hawker Sea Hawk FGA.4 WV798 received the attentions of Sydenham in 1963.

DH Sea Venom FAW.22 XG724 was at RNAY Sydenham twice in the 1960s.

DH Sea Devon XJ322 was at RNAY Sydenham between 1971 and 1973. (all Raymond Burrows Collection)

DH Sea Vixen XJ607 at an Aldergrove Air Display. (Tommy Maddock)

Left: Royal Navy Buccaneers of 736 NAS at a Sydenham Open Day in May 1969. (Irish News)

Hartland Point and Maidstone at Sydenham 1973. (Belfast Telegraph)

Army vehicles at Sydenham in 1971. (Author's Collection)

Devons, Sea Princes and Buccaneers. In a lean period, "repair lines were set up for bedsteads, fire extinguishers and other assorted bits of ironmongery." An apprentice training centre was set up in 1964.

In October 1969, Airport Wharf came into use again, this time as the berth for the accommodation (and sometime prison) ship HMS *Maidstone*, which was joined by RFA *Hartland Point*. Sydenham became a tri-service establishment with a large influx of army

Top: Sioux XT 202 operated with Kangaw Flight at Sydenham in 1972. (Eric Myall)

Middle: Scouts from 45 Commando flew from Long Kesh in 1974. (Eric Myall)

Bottom: Gazelle XX 413/R of 3CBAS visiting Sydenham on 3rd November 1976. (Raymond Burrows)

personnel. On the other side of the airfield, a safe haven was provided from time to time for up to 1000 Belfast Corporation buses, bin lorries and other heavy vehicles, which otherwise were a soft target for rioters. Along with the rest of the Province, the workers at Sydenham coped with the onset of renewed civil strife, the bombs and hoaxes, the shootings and strikes, while maintaining as much of the pattern of everyday life as possible. In 1971, following the closure of HMS *Sea Eagle*, Sydenham, now the centre of naval activity in Northern Ireland, once more became entitled to fly the White Ensign. In the same year a new task was added, work on mechanical components for the RAF and RN's Phantom fighters. By 1972 the military population had reached 3000, including Moscow Camp on the former engine test bed site. Airport Wharf came into use as a forward operating base for naval vessels patrolling Northern Irish waters.

Wessex HU5 from 707 NAS RFA Resource Flt which operated from Sydenham in 1977. (Pat Hindley)

In July 1973 the RN relinquished the site to the RAF and so the station became Royal Air Force Sydenham. It was home to a succession of Royal Marine Commando and Army Air Corps Sioux detachments from February 1973 until August 1976, thereafter the final two tours were undertaken by the Gazelles of 3 Commando Brigade Air Squadron, until the withdrawal from this base in October 1977. Earlier in 1977 the deployment of Wessex HU Mk5 had been given a trial by the RFA *Resource* Flight, which was part of 707 NAS. The aircraft operated from Sydenham.

The helicopters of the Royal Marines performed similar duties to those of the Army Air Corps, light liaison duties and surveillance in urban areas. To complete the picture with regard to RM helicopters, Sioux of 45 Commando were based at Aldergrove in the summer of 1970 and again briefly in 1972, as were the Sioux of 42 Commando. Scouts from 45 Commando flew from the old wartime airfield at Long Kesh in 1974. The memories of David Llewelyn Davies set out below may be regarded as typical of the period.

Kangaw Flight of 3 Commando Brigade Air Squadron arrived at Sydenham on 14th February 1972. The Flight Commander was Captain JD Llewelyn Davies RM, the other pilots deployed were Sergeant Porter RM and Sergeant Hunter PARA. The three Sioux were XT515, XT213 and XT202. Accommodation was provided on board HMS *Maidstone*. Most of the flying was in the Belfast - Lisburn area. Captain Llewelyn Davies handed over command to Lieutenant PM Wray RM on 9th March. He was operational in British Honduras five days later and returned to Ulster later in the year. He arrived at Aldergrove on 9th August 1972 along with Sergeant Skennerton RM and Sergeant Hunter PARA. The three Sioux, XT515, XT213 and XT844 took six hours and thirty-six minutes to fly from Coypool via Filton, Staverton, Speke, Carlisle and West Freugh. The first operational sortie was flown the next day, carrying the Commander Royal Engineers NI Land Forces in XT213 from Lisburn to Londonderry, Eglinton, Ballykelly, Creggan and back to Lisburn. The deployment came to an end on 2nd September. During the two deployments the Flight mainly either flew, stood by or slept.

Sydenham was developed as Belfast Harbour Airport from February 1983, being renamed Belfast City Airport in 1989, adding George Best to the title in 2006.

ALDERGROVE

Following the successful trial based at Sydenham mentioned above, the first FAA unit to be based at Aldergrove since 774 NAS in 1939-40 was a detachment of four 845 NAS Wessex HU Mk5s from October 1977 to May 1982. These aircraft, which were very similar to the RAF's HC Mk2s, spent much of their time either flying between Aldergrove and Bessbrook in County Armagh or carrying out tasks from the base at Bessbrook Mill. Personnel served tours of six weeks in duration, in a two year tour this could mean five or six spells in the Province. In the late 1970s a regular routine was moving a patrol of eight troops around the perimeter of Aldergrove to ensure the security of the base. Night time operations at that time, before the introduction of night vision goggles (NVG) could be very challenging, particularly in the marginal weather conditions often encountered in the scenic hills and dales of South Armagh. On arrival at Bessbrook in the late afternoon for "night-cab" duties, the first task would be to make a reconnaissance of that night's landing sites before the light faded. Navigation was by map, compass and stop

845 NAS Wessex HU5 over Londonderry in August 1980. (Belfast Telegraph)

91

watch with an Army Air Corps Gazelle overhead to illuminate the landing site with its powerful Nite-Sun at the appropriate moment. The many high tension cables strung across the countryside were an additional hazard. There is no doubt that naval pilots carried out many feats requiring great airmanship skills, courage and determination, particularly when recovering wounded Army or RUC personnel. On one occasion a government minister was being taken on a routine trip to visit bases when a Royal Marines unit suffered heavy casualties in a mortar attack at Crossmaglen. The minister opted to stay on board and witness the lengthy and difficult casualty evacuation. Back at Aldergrove after a much longer series of flights than he had anticipated that morning, he thanked the young RN pilot for, "The most enlightening experience I have ever had." Another pilot from the same squadron was engaged in lifting a cow which had been stranded in a bog by means of a strop underslung from the helicopter when they came under fire from across the Border – whether the target was the cow or the helicopter is not known but both survived without injury. There was plenty of flying for the aircrews, usually about 75 hours per tour. The Squadron reported in 1980,

> "Life on our main front has been fairly routine with the Senior Service being publicised during the 10th Anniversary of the formation of the Ulster Defence Regiment and a SAR incident concerning a small boat's occupants who succeeded in capsizing their craft in front of the Larne ferry. We also sent an aircraft to the Irish Republic with a member of the Northern Ireland Office for discussions with members of the Eire Government. Selection for this trip was made by using the old adage of needing at least 1000 hours, a green rating and having been there before. The Detachment Commander was unanimously selected!"

In August 1980 aid was given to the civil community in Londonderry in connection with repairs to a cathedral spire. Another less routine form of duty took place in 1980-81 when a naval Lynx of HMS *Ambuscade* Flight, 815 NAS painted in Army colours, carried out coastal patrols looking for gun runners. 845 NAS reported in 1982, "Not all detachments can be to the sun and our all-green Wessex continue to appear in all parts of the United Kingdom. In Northern Ireland, in the temporary absence of No.72 Squadron RAF, we are being kept very busy by the Army and the Royal Marines." 72 also operated the venerable but much loved Wessex and the two squadrons got on well together in the mess, where one of the popular pastimes to initiate new members (regardless of rank) was

Lynx HAS2 XZ691 of 815 NAS at Aldergrove in 1980-81. (Pat Hindley)

to throw them out the window into the rose bushes – luckily from the ground floor.

The Wessex HU Mk5s were followed by the Sea King HC Mk 4s of 707 NAS in 1993-94 and those of 846 NAS from 1994 to 1999 and again in 2001 and 2002. Usually two and sometimes three aircraft were detached to Aldergrove. One Sea King flew the night shift out of Bessbrook, while the other was available for Province wide tasking during the daylight hours. A 24 hour spell of duty at Omagh was also a regular feature in the first part of the decade. The availability of NVG equipment was a great boon. These medium support helicopters performed essentially the same function as the RAF's Wessex and Puma of Nos 33, 72 and 230 Squadrons. The normal jobs included carrying stores, equipment and personnel to the hilltop forts or inserting and picking up patrols in the field. The Sea King HC Mk 4 was a development of the naval anti-submarine version which was also manufactured by Westlands. The outboard floats, radar and ASW equipment were removed and a tactical transport helicopter was created which could carry up to 28 troops, 2722 kg (6000 lbs) internally or an underslung load of 3628 kg (8000 lbs). It could be said that there was a certain amount of inter-service rivalry between the Sea King and Puma crews. The Sea King was not as fast as a Puma and not quite as manoeverable in the air but in all other ways it was the ideal aircraft for the job. It had better range and endurance and could carry more. It was rugged enough to land in almost any spot and could fit into all the landing sites. It did not need time to re-role from carrying stores internally to underslung loading. The Sea King liked being worked hard, the more it flew the better it kept running. It was very popular with the troops on the ground but this is probably also due to the RN Commando Helicopter Force's "can do" attitude. They knew that if it was humanly possible the Navy would be there. It was felt by the naval pilots that the operating procedures under which the RAF had to work were a little more restrictive than the Navy's – for example a naval pilot could be more flexible with crew duty time in the case of an emergency. The RN guidance stated that crews should not plan to fly more than eight hours in a 24 hour period rather than have it set in stone as an absolute. Royal Marines aircrew, of course, served in and continued to fly Commando Force helicopters throughout the period.

That there was – at times – something of an edge to this rivalry can be seen from the following poem written by a naval pilot. It was less then well received by the RAF at Aldergrove and a copy of it now hangs on the wall in a crewroom at Yeovilton.

Tigger's Tale

When Tigger the Puma came to play,
As duty helo at BBK,
All the soldiers began to moan,
"Oh No" they said, "we'll never get home!"

"Oh gloom" they dripped, "They've sent us Tigger",
"What we need is something bigger",
"Hello Zero, do something",
If only SHFNI had sent a King

Moggy puffed and tried to prove,
these eight young soldiers he could move,
"I'll show them I'm no wussy"
Said our fearless stripey pussy

But as the wheels began to get light,
The man on the sticks took a sudden fright,
For there in the skies he could plainly see,
A big dark cloud over Tandragee

"Oh dash" said the pilot, "we'll have to go",
"We're way out of limits Tiggs, don't you know",
"Come on old Puss, the bar's open at eight",
"Sod 'em, they're squaddies, they'll have to wait"

Poor 'ole Tiggs held his head in shame,
"No wonder we Pumas have such a bad name",
"I only want to finish one task,
Is that really too much to ask?"

One forty knots North, job incomplete,
"Home by six Tiggs, oh what a feat",
"Troops still in the field, oh what a shame",
"Not my problem mate, I'll just pass the blame"

So off the troops yomped with hopes forlorn,
"Ten miles to go, we'll be back by dawn",
"The crabs get the job done, that'll be the day",
"How much do they get for their flying pay?"

With the cloud on the deck this dark night,
A helo now would be a welcome sight,
On and on yomped the weary men,
Home tonight would be Crossmaglen

In the hangar that night Tiggs sat all glum,
With Willy the Wessex, his dear old chum,
"Willy, 'tis the pilots" he did confide,
"They've loads of rules, but sod all pride"

All: Sea Kings in action in Northern
Ireland (Author's Collection via
David Green)

But out in the field the cougar called with glee,
"Sea King inbound, with you in three",
From out of the night the King roared out loud,
"Thank God for the Navy, they've done us proud"

So listen you all of RAF fame,
You're here for a job, it's not just a game,
So here's the point lads, remember one thing,
Put your Fear in God, but Honour the KING!!

Loads carried by the Sea King varied in composition from fuel to sewage (externally) to personnel and stores (internally). Perhaps one of the oddest underslung loads was a much anticipated Space Invaders machine for the entertainment of the troops stationed at Forkhill. Sadly it struck the perimeter fence on approach, denting the sturdy rocket proof barrier but

RN Sea King with underslung load somewhere between Aldergrove and Bessbrook.
(RAF Aldergrove)

Sea Kings in South Armagh. (David Green)

writing off the machine. Another underslung load of waste from Newtownhamilton caused a problem one day – strain as it might the Sea King could not lift what looked like an innocuous pile of cardboard. It was discovered that the soft but persistant South Armagh rain had soaked in to such an extent that the weight had been trebled. 12 to 16 was the usual number of troops carried, the standard patrol being 12 soldiers, a policeman and a dog. Police or Army sniffer dogs were popular with the aircrews. One day a friendly aircrewman offered the dog an extra strong mint, which was gobbled up. That, as the handler pointed out, was the end of the dog's usefulness for the day, as its sensory organ could now only smell mint. Another dog, a beautiful chocolate labrador, which was used to the routine, jumped onto the aircrewman's seat by the port blister window. The dog looked out of the window and then down at the map several

Sniffer dogs were populat with the aircrews. (David Green)

A Sea King at Drumcree with RUC Mobile Support Unit personnel emerging. (Niall Griffin)

times – obviously ready for action. From the late 1990s the church and surrounding area at Drumcree became a regular summer duty for the annual stand-off between the Security Forces and the Orangemen. The Sea King normally worked out of Portadown during this event, ready to deploy a Mobile Support Unit of policemen. Apparently much of the chat from the RUC/PSNI concerned the overtime they were earning and how they proposed to spend it. One protestor at Drumcree was quite innovative, he brought a pitching wedge and a supply of golf balls, with which he attempted to hit either the helicopter or policemen. Crews enjoyed coming to Ulster, it was a great learning environment to develop tactical flying and mission management skills in what were often marginal weather conditions. Navigational skills were also enhanced by the need avoid incursions across the twisting and tortuous 303 mile border with the Irish Republic. The final day of operations from Aldergrove was 16th October 2002, the RN kept going right to the end, the Detachment Commander recorded nine and a half hours flying in his log book.

Sea King from HMS Gannet Prestwick. (RN)

The story of naval aviation in Northern Ireland had come to an end, at least for the time being, apart from the odd sortie by Sea Kings of 771 NAS from Prestwick on an air-sea rescue mission. The last Sea King based at Aldergrove departed in 2002, Eglinton ceased to be a naval air station nearly 50 years ago and it is improbable that naval aircraft will ever be constructed at Bombardier

Aerospace, Sydenham (formerly Short Brothers) or that a ship capable of carrying naval aircraft will be built by the rump that is left of Harland and Wolff - the last such was Ship No.1727, the Royal Fleet Auxiliary *Fort Victoria* completed in 1992. Only memories remain, the best part of a century of service which was also of great economic benefit to the community.

RFA Fort Victoria (David Bolton)

Other aviation capable ships associated with Northern Ireland have included:

(above left) HMS Engadine on a visit to Londonderry in March 1968. (David Hill)

(above right) HMS Fearless was built in Belfast and launched in 1965. (Author's Collection)

(left) The MV Contender Bezant was rebuilt as the aviation training ship RFA Argus in 1984-87 and is seen here in the north Arabian Gulf in the primary hospital receiving role with a medical party of Royal Marine Bandsmen unloading casualties on the flight deck. (George Gardiner)

POSTSCRIPT

— ∞ —

History, of course, is out of date as soon as it is written. Just as the typescript of this book was being finalised, there was a further addition to the story of naval aviation in the Province. On 6th September 2006, a Westland Lynx HAS Mk 3S, XZ696, from the Operational Readiness Unit (ORU), which is part of 815 NAS at RNAS Yeovilton, arrived at RAF Aldergrove, crewed by Lieutenant Pete Higgins and Lieutenant Nigel Roberts. Its purpose was to help replace some of the capability lost by the withdrawal of 230 Squadron's Pumas from tasking in Northern Ireland (in future the Pumas will all be available for overseas duties and will confine their activities in Ulster to training). The Lynx's role was to act as the daytime Province utility aircraft. This consisted chiefly of the insertion and

RN Lynx HMA8 on a good-will visit to the Irish Air Corps at Baldonnel in May 2004. (Irish Air Corps)

Lynx HAS 3S XZ696 arriving at Braniel Primary School in late Autumn 2006. (via Steve Carroll)

collection of patrols in South Armagh; it has a very similar capability to the Army Lynx Mk 7, being able to carry six fully equipped troops. Another task is assisting the PSNI in the secure transportation of blasting explosives (by underslung load) for quarry operators. The Lynx can uplift between 680 and 1360 kilograms (1500 and 3000 lbs) underslung. There has also been time for school visits in support of the Directorate of Naval Recruiting (DNR), for training with submarines as they work up in the Clyde area and for liaison with the University Royal Naval Unit in Liverpool. After six weeks the original crew was replaced by, Lieutenant Commander Andy Hurry (the Officer in Charge of the ORU) and Lieutenant Ali Lang. This deployment came to an end in December 2006. Given the historical association of 815 NAS with Northern Ireland it is highly appropriate that a detachment of four Lynx will be based at Aldergrove from April 2007 until the end of Operation Banner in August 2007, according to current plans as of January 2007. 815's close connection with Northern Ireland goes back some sixty years. It was re-formed at Eglinton on three occasions with Barracuda IIIs in 1947 (re-equipping with Avengers in 1953), with Gannets in 1956 and with Whirlwinds in 1958.

It is also anticipated that naval helicopters will visit Northern Ireland regularly in support of DNR, as was the case recently when a Sea King ASaC Mk 7 from 849 NAS came over to undertake a series of school visits.

Another welcome visitor to schools in counties Antrim and Down in 2006, was this Sea King ASaC Mk 7. (via Steve Carroll)

BIBLIOGRAPHY

Books

Allison, RS, HMS Caroline, The Blackstaff Press, Belfast 1974

Brand, Stanley, Achtung! Swordfish! Merchant Aircraft Carriers, Propagator Press, Leeds, 2005

Francis, Dermot, Lacey, Brian and Mullen, Jim, Atlantic Memorial The Foyle and the Western Approaches 1939-45, Derry City Council, Heritage & Museum Service

Gardner, Richard E, The Flying Navy, Almark Publications, New Malden, 1971

James, Derek N, Westland A History, Tempus Publishing Ltd., Stroud, 2002

Kilbracken, John, Bring back my Stringbag, Pen & Sword Books Ltd., Barnsley, 1996

MacCarron, Donal, Landfall Ireland, Colourpoint Books, Newtownards, 2003

McDougal, Flight Lieutenant JS, Greig JB and Baird WA, A History of RAF Sydenham 1939-1978, RAF Sydenham, Belfast, 1978

Moss, Michael and Rune, John R, Shipbuilders to the World 125 Years of Harland and Wolff, Belfast 1861-1986, The Blackstaff Press, Belfast, 1986

Ronkes, FH and Sjoukema, J, De Historic Van Marine Vliegkamp de Kooy & Vliegtuig Squadron 860, Netherlands Institute for Military History, 1983

Sturtivant, Ray and Page, Gordon, Royal Navy Aircraft Serials and Units 1911-1919, Air-Britain (Historians) Ltd., Tonbridge 1992

Sturtivant, Ray and Balance, Theo, The Squadrons of the Fleet Air Arm, Air-Britain (Historians) Ltd., Tonbridge 1994

Vicary, Adrian, Naval Wings Royal Naval carrier-borne aircraft since 1916, Patrick Stephens Ltd., Cambridge, 1981

Warner, Guy, Airships over the North Channel, Ulster Aviation Society, Belfast, 2005

Warner, Guy and Woods, Jack, In the Heart of the City - the History of Belfast's City Airport 1938-98, Adleader Publications, Belfast 1998.

Warner, Guy and Woods, Jack, Belfast International Airport - Aviation at Aldergrove since 1918, Colourpoint Books, Newtownards 2001.

Wragg, David, Royal Navy Handbook 1939-1945, Sutton Publishing, Stroud, 2005

Wragg, David, Stringbag The Fairey Swordfish at War, Pen & Sword Books Ltd., Barnsley, 2004

Newspapers and Periodicals

Aeroplane, Air Pictorial, Airfield Review Extra, Belfast Newsletter, Belfast Telegraph, Flight, Flight Deck, Friends of the Eighth Newsletter, Irish News, Navy News, RAF Flying Review, Shorts Quarterly Review, Ulster Airmail

The author wishes to express his grateful thanks to: Mike Abbey, John Beattie, Dick Beechener, Kathleen Bell, Mark Bentinck, Ken Best, Stanley Brand, Tom Brown, Martin Browning, Mick Burrow, Ray Burrows (for his expert advice and proof-reading), Eddie Cadden, Steve Carroll, Paul Carson, Sir Desmond Cassidi, Mike Caws, Ernie Cromie, David Llewelyn Davies, Seamus Devine, John Emrick, Maurice Fitzgerald, George Gardiner, David Gibbings, Eric Gray, David Green, Niall Griffin, John Hamlin, David Hill (for his great assistance with the selection of photographs), Pat Hindley, Joe Honywill, Andy Hurry, David "Jimmy" James, ERA "Johnny" Johnson, Tom Joyce, Paul Kriebel, Alan Lamb, Alisdair Lang, Mike Lewis, Keith Lloyd, Joan Long (née Feather), Andrew Marshall, Donal MacCarron, Lawrie McCarthy, Sandy McClearn, John McDonald, Nat McGlinchey, Hugh McGrattan, Don MacGregor, Alan McKnight, Paul McMaster, Peter Monte, Harry Morley, David Morrissey, Eddie Murray, Eric Myall, Eddie Parker, Will Penkman, Alfred Price, Geoff Richardson, Peter Richardson, Catherine Rounsfell, Richard Seymour, Jerry Shore, Nick Stroud, Ray Sturtivant, Barry Wheeler, Tony Wilson, George White, David Wragg, David Wright, Navy News, Flight Deck, Fleet Air Arm Officers Association, Fleet Air Arm Museum, RN Submarine Museum.